C000151990

THE GOD OF
PAGE ONE

Other titles from Freddy Hedley

Listening for Mission
(with Steve Croft and Bob Hopkins)

Lessons from Antioch

Coaching for Missional Leadership
(with Bob Hopkins)

A Pioneer's Understanding of the Church
(with Bob Hopkins)

The Lost Story: The Scroll of Remembrance

Walking in Freedom

The Eden Complex
(due for publication, Spring 2013)

English Standard Version

THE GOD OF PAGE ONE

Rediscovering God's identity and ours

FREDDY HEDLEY

emblembooks

www.emblembooks.co.uk

Published in the United Kingdom by Emblem Books.

Unless otherwise indicated, biblical quotations are taken from the English Standard Version (ESV) © 2001 by Crossway Bibles.

ISBN 978-0-9559594-5-5

Cover design by MPH.

This first edition published in 2012 by Emblem Books

www.emblembooks.co.uk

For Ali, Maisie and Isobel

CONTENTS

ACKNOWLEDGEMENTS

I have no solitary claim over anything in this book, since it has all emerged along a journey I have shared with others. It is easy to forget, since so much of the actual time invested in writing this was done in a room on my own; however, none of these words would have been possible were it not for the ideas sparked by conversations and studies, the refining of understanding through the same and access to the seemingly limitless wisdom of my family, friends and colleagues.

This covers a lot of people very anonymously, and if you find yourself in one or more of these camps - thank you! However, there are a few individuals I particularly want to acknowledge.

First, there is no-one who has had a bigger impact on this material than Ali, my wife, who has endured musings, ponderings and general spouting off as I have shaped this material out loud, always with gracious patience and the willingness to chip in, correct and challenge, so that she has contributed hugely to what came out of the other end.

And of course, behind her - and often, on top of her - are our two lovely girls, Maisie and Isobel, who have had remarkably little to say on the matter, but then they are only six and (very nearly) two years old so perhaps it is only to be expected. I love you all.

But there are many others. I owe so much to Stephen Mawditt, minister at Fountain of Life Church in Ashill, Norfolk, where my family and I are based and where I am privileged to serve. His willingness to release me into a ministry of teaching here has led to so much of this material being developed, as have all the ad hoc conversations along the way. His leadership, vision and friendship are all major factors in your reading these words now.

My colleagues at Westminster Theological Centre have also played a big part in the development of this material, whether directly through the extraordinary teaching of the faculty or indirectly through the fellowship and discipleship of the staff team. Particular thanks are due to Crispin Fletcher-Louis, Peter Fitch and Jo Pestell, for their kindness in proof-reading, affirming, challenging and correcting my words, and to Bob Ekblad, whose teaching (in addition to Crispin and Peter) also contributed to how I have thought about the material in this book.

And then there are the many friends at Fountain of Life who made their valuable contribution by helping me to shape this material in teaching sessions, ad hoc conversations, proof reading and feedback, through their general willingness to affirm and challenge my words, and occasionally to teach it in my absence!

In particular I want to name Adam Jackson, Phil Starling, Dave Blane, the amazing FoL interns and the equally inspiring WTC students.

Thanks also go to my oldest friends and brothers in arms: Tom, Nige and Paul who, even when they don't get to influence the material I am working on, continue to influence the man I am becoming, and so I want to thank them for everything I produce.

Almost lastly, thank you to everyone at Fountain of Life Church and the Fountain Network for being the nursery where these ideas were birthed and raised.

Thank you all!

And actually lastly, I must acknowledge that in thanking Ali I told a lie, because there is one significant person who has had a far bigger impact and influence on all of this material.

Thank you, Jesus.

September 2012

HOW TO USE THIS BOOK

WHAT I have tried to do in this book is to present the journey of discovery I have undertaken in my studies of Genesis 1, as well as my final conclusions. Reflecting this, the opening two chapters explore the foundations that underpin this study, as well as the issues I was wrestling with that led to my getting started, and the principles which lie behind my approach to study and so determined everything I go on to describe.

Then, with each of the following chapters, I have started by presenting the questions that first challenged and opened the passage up for me as I was gathering my thoughts for how I would teach and write this material, before finally presenting my conclusions in the body of the chapter.

There are, therefore, a number of ways you could approach this book. On the one hand, it is just a book: you start at the beginning, read your way through to the end, and it either impacts you or it doesn't. However, there is also the opportunity to engage more directly with the material.

Occasionally throughout the text I have left space for notes and the study questions at the start of each chapter also have space for your own reflections.

This might be something that is done privately, or with others. In particular the study questions could be used as the basis for bible study, whether that is one study, where you take the 'key question' I have highlighted in each chapter, or whether you follow this book as a study series, taking a chapter or two each time.

To help with this, I have limited the number of questions I have offered to only three or four. I don't want to give you a resource that asks so many questions that it robs you of the time to properly explore them, and denies you the space to ask your own questions. I would also hate you to think there were "right" answers you were aiming for, which might stifle your own view.

Personally, I believe bible study should be more about asking questions than reaching answers, and more about discovery than direction so I want to encourage you to ask questions beyond the ones I have presented and to have the freedom to stop on one issue and explore it as far as you or your group want, particularly when it takes you into application and prayer.

With this in mind, I have also highlighted one question in each study as a 'key question', which may help you to decide which issues to prioritise in a flowing discussion, or which questions to ask should you want to cover all of Genesis 1 in one session.

However you engage with this material, I hope and pray it is a blessing to you.

1

WHAT'S THE STORY?

Man does not live by bread alone,
but man lives by every word that comes
from the mouth of the LORD.

Deuteronomy 8 v 3

THE BIBLE is a very short book.

I can almost hear the objections from here: 'Surely not! It takes years to read!' Or, 'But it's more than a thousand pages!'

True enough. To be precise, if you were to read one chapter a day it would take three and a quarter years to read, and the English Standard Version (ESV) copy that I have on the table beside me as I write this runs to 1,392 pages, with text so small I have to peer closely into the pages to read it.

In fact, while we're at it, let's bring out a few more choice statistics.

This is not one book at all, but sixty-six. The word 'bible' derives from the Greek 'ta biblia' which means 'The books'[1] - literally a library. Gathered together it contains two testaments, with thirty-nine books in the old and twenty-seven in the new.

---

[1] Douglas Harper, *Bible*, Online Etymology Dictionary (www.etymonline.com)

All told there are 1,189 chapters, 31,103 verses and (for the ESV) 757,000 words. That's more than 200,000 words longer than *War and Peace* or *The Lord of the Rings* and is longer than the first six *Harry Potter* books combined.

You might well accuse me of playing very loose with the definition of 'short.' But I stick to my statement. The Bible is a very short book indeed.

Think for a moment what this book is trying to convey. If you read *War and Peace*, you are treated to an expansive narrative of the rise and fall of Russia during the Napoleonic Wars, following the intimate details of several families, mostly the social elite, covering up to three generations, set amid two interweaving storylines of life in peaceful Russia and life on the brutal frontline of battle.

It is an extraordinary achievement, spanning eight years from 1805 to 1813, and yet it still feels condensed at 560,000 words. The Bible is only a third longer and yet it intimately follows the history of God and His people across thousands of years, including detailed accounts of their highs and lows, their spiritual, social, political and military make-up, plus many intimate portrayals of individuals, written as history, law, letters, poetry, song, proverb and prophecy.

Already its achievement surpasses any novel, and this is before we have even begun to acknowledge the most important aspect.

THE BIG STORY

Not too long ago (as I write this in Spring 2012) I was leading a bible study session with the interns at Fountain of Life Church in Norfolk, where I am based, and I asked them the most unfair question I could think of in the moment: how would you summarise The Bible's primary purpose in one sentence?

I was expecting: "What?! That's 757,000 words, condensed into maybe 15?!" What I got was all I probably deserved: four mildly troubled, disapproving faces, followed by some really great answers - but they were all too long!

It is an unfair enough question at the best of times, but all the more so given that I gave them no notice so they had to answer off the cuff, and even more unfair because it was very clearly a leading question. I had obviously given this quite a bit of thought, so they knew I probably had an answer I was hoping to get to.

I have since asked this question many times in teaching sessions and it has always led to a fruitful exploration of how we value God's Word, and often led to some great insights, but rarely do we get it down to one sentence! And this excites me, because the reason we can't do it is almost always because the discussion alone sparks a passion for how amazing a book this is and once we start sharing what we think it is saying, it can be difficult to stop.

And yet, when left to our own devices, so many of us struggle to come to God's Word with the same sense of enthusiasm. Sometimes we can become too familiar with The Bible in isolation, so that its words take root in the one way we have always read them privately and they come to seem one dimensional, leaving us immune to hearing God in fresh ways.

In which case, there is no better tonic than sitting down with others and digging into this question - what is it *for*? - and getting fired up all over again by what an exciting, dynamic, awe-inspiring, intimate, persuasive, wise, fascinating, revealing, challenging, informative, powerful, life-changing, book this is. The more words the better!

But sometimes words can be distracting as well as inspiring, and what we need is to ponder the most fundamental urgencies of The Bible's message, to draw our eye back to the very centre of the Father's heart, to capture its essence in a glance. The fewer words the better.

So let me lay the unfair question at your door. How would you summarise The Bible's primary purpose in one sentence? Perhaps this is a moment to put this book down and wrestle with this question, either alone or with friends.

See if you can get it down to less than twenty words.

NOTES

The Bible ...

My suggestion - and it is only a suggestion - is this: The Bible reveals who God is, who we are and how we relate together.

It goes without saying that The Bible speaks to many other things as well. There are passages that speak to different aspects of lifestyle, values for living, comments about the world, social action, justice, mission strategy, and so on. But as these passages do this, they all seek to reveal who God is, who we are and how we relate together. It is all about identity and relationship.

Compared to these, nothing else matters, because it is these revelations that underpin the purpose of creation, the pursuit of covenant, the power of the cross and the promise of Christ's kingdom. No matter how many other things it sheds light on along the way, the primary purpose of The Bible at all times is to drive us towards these three revelations and every word makes its contribution.

This is the heart of The Bible's big story, the meta-narrative: the one seam that draws the whole together. From the first words of Genesis to the last words of Revelation, this is the story of how God set aside space for us to be together.

It is God's story and it is our story, in all its fullness. It is at once an intimate love story and an epic war drama, a socio-political thriller and an exhilarating adventure, a devastating tragedy and the most joyous good news.

Quite simply, it is the greatest story ever told.

WHAT'S THE STORY?

Within the pages of this book is contained the complete revelation of an eternal, all-powerful, all-knowing, unfathomable God, giving us everything we need to know to have a deep and meaningful relationship with Him: His character, His loves, His hates, His behaviour, His deepest desires, the lengths He goes simply to be with those He loves above all else, the sacrifices He has made, the great battles He has fought and will fight, and the best happily-ever-after ending that has ever been conceived.

Within these pages is contained the deepest portrayal of humanity in all its frailty and all its brilliance, in all its worthlessness and all its inestimable value. We find ourselves to be the worst of sinners and yet the image of God, and heirs to the King of kings; too often a host for evil and yet also the dwelling place of the Holy Spirit, the Temple of God, and the most beloved bride of Christ.

Within these pages we see the fullness of God's love for us, His hopes for us, His desire to extend His Kingdom and change the world through us, and more than all of that, His deepest desire to reclaim that space set aside for us to be together. We see how this relationship - God's ultimate vision both for Him and for us - was briefly possible but then corrupted; how it was patched over and then finally restored completely.

And it manages to do all this in a mere 1,392 pages. This really is a very short book indeed.

HIDDEN TREASURE

In a book as short as this there is no room for waste, no space for unnecessary words. And yet I regularly find myself skipping over bits as I read them. Be honest, you know the bits I'm talking about: the lists of names, the unpronounceable names, the repetition[2], the unfamiliar language, the beginnings and ends of letters.

We've all struggled to engage with these passages. I've even heard them described as "the boring bits." In fact, now I come to think about it, it may very well have been me that called them that!

And then I think about the things that are not in The Bible, such as all the teaching of Jesus that none of the Gospel writers saw fit or found space to include.

John says at the end of his book:

> *Now there are also many other things that Jesus did. Were every one of them to be written, I suppose that the world itself could not contain the books that would be written.*

John 21 v 25

John almost seems to tease us with the thought that Jesus did and said so much more than we know. We think we have a complete picture of Jesus, but if we

---

[2] Why, for example, does Exodus 36-39 repeat Exodus 25-28 almost verbatim - why not just say 'God's people did exactly as He said?' Why?!

take John's word for it, then we must barely know him at all. Or at least, we barely know what he said and did.

Do you remember John Lennon's comment in 1965 about The Beatles being bigger than Jesus? Well, there are books available now that describe literally The Beatles every movement for the first half of their career, during 'Beatlemania.'[3] They may not be bigger than Jesus, but it seems they are better documented!

Surely the life and words of Jesus are sufficiently important to have been given more page space? He is, after all, the cornerstone of our faith, God incarnate, and his every word and action was a revelation of God's love and power.

Couldn't John - or Matthew, Mark or Luke for that matter - have included just a little bit more? If it was a question of space in The Bible, surely a few of those lists of names earlier on could have been sacrificed! I wonder how much else is not there that I, in my limited wisdom, would have included over and above "the boring bits."

Of course, if I regain my perspective, and remind myself that my limited wisdom really is very limited indeed compared with the infinite wisdom of The Bible's editor-in-chief (see 2 Timothy 3 v16), then I must concede that there is only one conclusion. The lists of names, the repetition, the beginnings and

---

[3] The particular tome on my bookshelf is *The Beatles: Ten Years That Shook The World* by Paul Trynka (Dorling Kindersley, 2004).

ends of letters, are all more important than the undocumented words and deeds of Jesus.

It almost sounds like heresy to say it, but it must be true. The Bible is God's Word and in its pages He has included everything we need to discover Him, to get to know Him fully, to see how we fit into His plans and to build a strong relationship with Him and out of that, with each other.

With so little space to cram this all in every word is precious. Every word must carry The Bible's meta-narrative forwards. There is only room for the gold seam, the richest of God's revelation, which will reveal God in all His glory, reveal us in all our significance and reveal the covenant relationship in all its grace. These are the revelations that set us free to take part in extending the frontiers of God's Kingdom, and which release the love of the Father.

The lists of names, the beginning and ends of letters, the repetitions, the unfathomable moments, all made the final cut. They all form the richest seam of revelation and invitation, to which the undocumented words of Jesus would not add.

If we see it in this light, suddenly we find ourselves with the most extraordinary opportunity to go back and ask new questions of The Bible. We can explore all the bits we've glanced over or ignored in the past, looking for new revelation in unexpected places, and we can revisit familiar passages, even old favourites, with renewed expectation. There is so much gold we have not yet mined!

WHAT'S THE STORY?

This change of mindset has had a profound impact on the way I read The Bible. My study times can no longer be separated into "routine" and "extraordinary," which if I am completely honest with you, was often how they used to be.

Now they are separated into fresh revelation (of the familiar) and new revelation (of the unfamiliar and the "boring bits"). I'm hitting the point now where I get really excited when I catch myself wanting to skip over a passage. The question has shifted from, "Urgh, Lord, why did you bother to include that?" to "Wow, Lord, why did you include that?! What revelation have I not yet tapped into?"

Let me give you an example. Take a moment to read Genesis 22 v20-24:

Now after these things it was told to Abraham, "Behold, Milcah also has borne children to your brother Nahor: Uz, his firstborn, Buz his brother, Kemuel the father of Aram, Chesed, Hazo, Pildash, Jidlaph, and Bethuel."
(Bethuel fathered Rebekah.)
These eight Milcah bore to Nahor, Abraham's brother. Moreover, his concubine, whose name was Reumah, bore Tebah, Gaham, Tahash, and Maacah.

Genesis 22 v 20-24

This comes immediately after the drama of Abraham's near sacrifice of his son Isaac to God, towards the end of the extraordinary account of Abraham's life. It is a wonderful moment of revelation, where Abraham's faith is rewarded by God making the sacrifice Himself (it's amazing really that Jesus was such a surprise when he came onto the scene!) and the virtues of trusting the Lord and watching for His grace and deliverance are reinforced.

At this pinnacle moment the action is interrupted and we are given this random short list of names: the descendents of Abraham's brother Nahor, about whom we are otherwise told absolutely nothing.

Having listed the names, the author of Genesis returns to Abraham's story as if nothing had happened, with no explanation as to why he saw fit to include them at all, let alone at this critical moment. It only seems to get in the way of the flow of revelation, so why put it there? It is a classic 'filler passage'! Well, let's take a moment to ponder what we know.

In Genesis 12 we read that Abraham had two brothers – Haran and Nahor. When Haran died responsibility for his son Lot passed to Abraham[4] and we follow in detail Abraham's amazing journey, his receiving of God's promise and Sarah's miraculous motherhood.

This takes many years and in all that time Nahor goes unnoticed. But then we learn in Genesis 22 that so many years have passed that by the time Sarah

---

[4] It is not specified, but presumably this indicates that Abraham was the older sibling; otherwise the charge would surely have passed to Nahor.

gives birth to Isaac, Abraham's younger brother has not only had time to have twelve children, but the youngest of his eight legitimate children has grown to adulthood and had children of his own, which include Rebekah.

Now it may be that in any given biblical list of names most of the names go over our head and leave us confounded, but we know Rebekah. If you were reading this for the very first time you wouldn't, of course, but it would not be long before you did, because a mere twenty-one verses later Rebekah becomes Isaac's wife, Abraham's daughter-in-law.

Do you see the significance? God's plan is perfect in every detail, and as such every branch in Jesus' family tree had to be precise for the outworking of the plan of salvation. Therefore, it was essential that, all those generations before, Isaac and Rebekah married. And the only way that was possible was for Sarah to wait two generations before having her first child.

There was no way Sarah could ever have seen this, and in a world where God's plan was revealed primarily through the order of His creation, I don't think we can reasonably criticise her faith for doubting that God would make her a mother. It is in no way unreasonable that an 89-year old woman struggled to believe that she would have children of her own! Indeed, given that her knowledge of God (and ours) started with Him being the creator of an ordered universe that was perfectly made, it was a faith*ful* assumption that this applied to her in her old age as much as it did for everything else.

We can have a tendency to read these accounts forgetting that these are real people being described. They are such established stories on the page that we see them as one-dimensional characters given to us to make a point, instead of real people with real problems, real expectations and real emotions, who chose to walk with God. So we remember Sarah as the character who laughed at the promise of God, and yet she believed in God's promise enough that she went to great lengths to see Abraham receive it.

Indeed, she demonstrated remarkable humility by stepping aside and offering her servant Hagar to Abraham, so that her husband could receive God's promise[5]. Surely this is a woman who believed that God's promise to Abraham was genuine, and who loved both God and her husband enough that she was prepared to do whatever it took, at whatever cost to herself, to see it happen.

Of course, it was still the wrong decision but then she had no way of seeing what God was planning. She thought her biggest dream was to have a child,

---

[5] This is not to say that she was giving up her rights or position in the family as the mother of Abraham's children. Archaeological studies suggest that the child would have been considered hers. But the Genesis account makes it clear that the influence of the natural mother was still powerful, which not only made Hagar a threat and cause of envy, but must have been a painful awareness for Sarah as she laid aside her own yearning for natural motherhood.

and so every day it didn't happen must have been a terrible weight of pain and disappointment. But God's biggest dream for her was that she would be the mother of the line of the King of kings - He intended Sarah to play a critical role in saving the whole of humanity and restoring creation.

God saw further, aimed higher and delivered far more than she could ever have imagined. Her mistake was not that she doubted God's promise was genuine, nor that she did not believe He could do amazing things; her mistake was to believe that He would not do them through her, and for her. This is where the frailty of her relationship with God is exposed, not in her natural doubt about her age.

It began with a fundamental misunderstanding of who God was: her personal God as well as her husband's, which in turn led to a fundamental misunderstanding of who she was - the woman God had chosen to start His line of kings, leading to His own son - which birthed a relationship built on the wrong foundations, so that despite her great faith, she was unable to hear the fullness of God's promise for her.

I have to say that what I see here is a woman whose faith looks an awful lot like mine and I am hugely encouraged to see that for all my limited perspective, I have a God who loves me more than I dare to believe, who has a perfect plan, and who is in the business of inviting me into having a far bigger impact in His creation than I will ever realise. And as I pursue that promise, what I learn from Sarah is the importance of rooting my relationship with God in learning more about who He is above all else.

As I say, this is a classic filler passage - one that many of us will have skipped over a dozen times without even noticing. But a closer examination reveals that, far from being a pointless tangent, this passage is one of the most essential links in the chain of God's plan for salvation.

My point is, there are no "boring bits" - no wasted words, no room for incidental tangents. The Bible is the most dynamic, exciting, fascinating book ever committed to paper. Its words are alive, they speak out God's voice, and every word sheds more light on who God is, who we are and how we can relate together.

I highlight this example from Abraham's life in particular because it takes us into the meta-narrative. Here we have an example of the author of Genesis taking a step back from the detail of Abraham's life, right at the moment when Isaac's place is established, to look at what is going on from a wider perspective, reminding us of God's unfolding plan, that He is in control of events and is doing something so much bigger than only giving Abraham and Sarah a son.

This is a list of names that is carefully placed. When you read them through for the first time it seems as though these names have been drawn out of nowhere and can fall back into nowhere without us remembering or worrying about them; but if we read them a second time, having read the rest of God's story, we find ourselves thinking, "I know who Rebekah is" and so the passage unfolds into the most extraordinary revelation of God as a master planner, of Sarah as a faithful servant who is crucial to God's plan for salvation, and to one of the first and most significant moments in time that contributes to the Temple curtain being torn in two so many hundreds of years later.

ASKING THE RIGHT QUESTIONS

So, how do we get to grips with The Bible's big story? The key, I think, is to be asking the right questions. Over the years I have seen so many discussions about the validity and message of The Bible get bogged down in conflicts which result from asking the questions 'when' and 'how.' Have you found the same?

When was the earth created? How was it done - literally as Genesis 1 describes, or figuratively? When will the earth come to an end? How will it happen - literally as Revelation describes, or figuratively? When was Jesus born - how can we believe he existed if we can't pinpoint this basic detail? How did he escape the tomb if not by resurrection? How does salvation work exactly - penal substitution, debt payment, or something else?

The questions go on and on, but sometimes it seems that they only take us round in circles. The problem is that The Bible is consistently vague about the questions of 'when' and 'how.' It doesn't see the need to explain the hidden mechanics of God's Kingdom, nor its timescales. Indeed, Jesus often urged us not to ponder such matters.

Take the end of the world as a case in point. Jesus says: "Do not be anxious about tomorrow, for tomorrow will be anxious for itself"[6]; "It is not for you know the times and seasons that the Father has fixed by his own authority"[7]; "Concerning that day and hour no one knows, not even the angels of heaven, nor the Son, but the Father only."[8] The message seems pretty clear: do not look for the end times - be ready now.

The result of this vagueness is that some people are dissatisfied with the mystery. So they seek to explain the secrets of God's Kingdom by picking up whatever clues they can from the limited material they have available to them.

I have read arguments from the cleverest and most committed scholars, theologians and scientists about all of the examples I mentioned just now - creation, end-times, salvation - and I struggle to find any two that precisely agree, because they are all relying on different 'clues' that they have found, be they scientific, literary, historical, theological or whatever.

Now I do not mean to criticise this process - or even to distance myself from it. In many ways, this book is

---

[6] Matthew 6 v34
[7] Acts 1 v7
[8] Matthew 24 v36

only me adding my voice to the crowd. Plenty of treasure has been uncovered by digging into these things, and yet still we find that the questions of 'when' and 'how' remain as unclear as ever.

It seems to me that The Bible is deliberately vague about these matters. And the only conclusion I can come to is that these are not the questions that are really going to open up the biblical meta-narrative to us, and therefore there simply isn't the room in so short a book to go into depth about them.

No doubt it would be fascinating to know for certain what the days of Genesis 1 really looked like, no doubt it would confirm our place in the universe, as the scientific world is so powerfully driven to do (and I say that in a spirit of considerable admiration); no doubt it would help our understanding to know for certain what really happened to our sin on the cross. But these are the mysteries of faith, and it can sometimes seem that we ask the 'when' and 'how' questions to try and absolve ourselves of the responsibility to have faith. The Bible is not going to let us off so easily!

Faith is the first evidence of a relationship with God[9], and a relationship with God is all God's Word is concerned about establishing. Unlocking the mysteries of faith runs the danger of diluting the integrity of that faith, and therefore weakening our relationship with God. This, I believe, is why the

---

[9] Hebrews 11 v6

'when' and 'how' issues are so often vague in The Bible.

Jesus describes true faith as being childlike (Matthew 18 v3). I have two young children. My eldest, Maisie, is six years old as I write this and, like all children of her age, she asks questions constantly. Or to be more precise, she asks one question repeatedly, and it isn't "How?"

It is, "Why?"

All children are fascinated by this question, and there seems to be no end to how far down they are willing to drill with this one penetrating word.

"Maisie, it's time for bed." (By which, of course, I mean I'm tired)

"Why?"

"Because you're tired." (By which, of course, I mean I'm tired)

"Why?"

"Because it's been a long day." (By which, of course, I mean I'm tired - can she not take this hint?)

"Why?"

"Because you have done so many things, been to school, played games, sung songs, read books and jumped on trampolines, and I don't think you've stopped once in twelve hours." (By which, of course, I mean I'm tired - really, do my heavy eyes and weary shoulders not give it away?!)

"Why?"

"Because you have so much energy." (By which, of course, I mean ... yes, you know)

"Why?"

"Because you love to do all those things."

"Why?"

"Because God made you that way."

"Why?"

"Because God loves those things too."

"Why?"

"Because having fun, reading books and jumping on trampolines are good things to do."

"Why?"

"Because they bring joy."

"Why?"

"Because ... err ... because I said so, now go to bed!"

I really want you to think I'm playing this up for effect, but I have had this conversation! "Why?" is a childlike faith question to ask, not "How?" The same goes for "When?" If I tell Maisie we are going to see some friends she does not want to know how long we are seeing them for, she wants to know *who* they are. When we are watching a film she is not interested in when it is set, she wants to know *who* the people are: are they real or pretend, are they good guys or bad guys, and so on.

Why and who: these are the first questions all children ask and these are the faith-filled questions we need to be asking of God's Word.

THE GOD OF PAGE ONE

There is a point in life, usually around the entry into secondary education and certainly with the onset of teenhood, when children are encouraged to stop asking why and who, and to begin asking how and when, and I find this a terrible shame, because I think it too often misdirects their fascination.

Sadly, as a society we prefer to throw these more innocent curiosities aside and measure adulthood against the ability to get things done. The consequence is that we live in a world governed by how and when - task oriented questions - at the expense of who and why - relationship and value oriented questions.

Exactly the same can be said of our faith. As we mature in Christ we can fall into the misunderstanding that 'growing up' means getting better at 'doing faith,' and so we focus on our identity as co-heirs on a journey towards Christ-likeness, expressed through faithful effort, where we will do even greater things than Jesus.

Obviously these are all entirely biblical and essential things to be holding close to our hearts, but the danger is that we can lose sight of the relationship at the expense of the responsibility, and when we do look at the relationship we can tend to see ourselves only as brothers and sisters (serving alongside) and forget that we are first and foremost sons and daughters (submitting before). In the face of eternity we are still the very young children of our Heavenly Father and so we need to retain our fascination with childlike questions.

If we have faith, we do not need to ask how and when (these are our Father's concerns), but we are free to ask who and why. And as soon as we ask these questions of The Bible, the answers begin to get very specific.

We don't know how the universe was created, how salvation works or how the world will end, but we can know who created the universe and why, who set humanity aside and why, who broke the relationship between God and humanity and why, and who restored that relationship and why.

In a snap shot, this is the biblical meta-narrative: God's and our big story, told in four momentous moments that shook the heavens and the earth, first casting and then completing God's vision for His and our life.

It begins with the creation of the universe, which reveals the Creator, followed by the singling out of humanity, which reveals our identity; then comes the breakdown in Eden, which reveals how the relationship was supposed to be and why it no longer seems that way; and finally comes the restoration of that relationship, first temporarily in Israel and ultimately through Jesus for all, which reveals how humanity can once again live in communion with God.

In this short book we are going to zoom in to closely examine the first of these moments, as well as touching on the second. Who is God and who are we? And as we ask these questions, we will also naturally find that from page one God's Word reveals his priority for relationship and what underpins it.

I will explore the remaining pivotal moments in God's story in the follow-up to this book[10], which I am in the process of completing as I write these words. However, to examine the whole meta-narrative in this one book would necessarily distract our attention from paying close enough attention to Genesis 1.

Therefore, for now, we are going to focus on considering how it all began - the creation of the universe, as told in Genesis 1 - and as we do this we must consider what The Bible's opening chapter has to say about who God is, who we are and how we relate together: the heart of God's story that unfolds over the following 1,391 pages.

But for now, let's not concern ourselves with those later pages. This book is only about the God we discover on page one.

BE FREE TO DISAGREE!

As we progress through, what I do not want to do is suggest that I am expounding the one and only true way to read Scripture. Indeed, I have no problem with you disagreeing with every word I say, so long

---

[10] Currently entitled *The Eden Complex: Exposing the roots of rules-driven faith and the relationship we should have had*, due to be published in Spring 2013.

as it spurs you towards God and seeking better answers!

So much that is good, challenging and powerful has been revealed by wiser people than I and I do not want to replace or imply correction to any of that light; but hopefully this book might add to it in some small way. It is important that we go into Scripture knowing there is always more to see and with the willingness to embrace the mystery, so I hope what we explore here together only adds light as we look at The Bible from the perspective of a listener to God's meta-narrative.

So, let's get started. Let's ask the 'who' and 'why' questions that can open up God's Word, and let's expect some very specific answers.

THE GOD OF PAGE ONE

2

A NOTE ON AUTHORSHIP

When you received the word of God ... you accepted it not as the word of men but as what it really is, the word of God.

1 Thessalonians 2 v 13

AS I have already indicated, I don't want our study in this book to get distracted by questions of 'when' and 'how', such as when was this passage written or how is it to be read - literally or not? However, I do think it would be helpful to pause for a moment before we dig in to consider authorship. Our first 'who' question.

Now, there are plenty of other books out there that cover this in more detail, from a much more solid base of knowledge than I have, so we will not linger here for long, but we ought to make sure we are clear on a couple of points.

It is relatively clear and pretty universally accepted these days that Genesis was not composed by one author. Traditionally, we ascribe this book in its entirety to Moses, as with the rest of the Pentateuch, and he may well have had a hand in telling it, may at a stretch even have written some of it for later generations to put together (though there really is no evidence for this - only the conjecture of hope!), but there is strong evidence to suggest at other voices prevailed and contributed to what we now understand to be God's final word in Genesis.

Essentially the evidence breaks down into matters of content and source material. In terms of content, Genesis is not written in one consistent style, which we might expect from one author. Given our focus for this book, let's take the two creation accounts of Genesis 1 and 2 as an example.

Consider how different they are in style. In Genesis 1, the seven days of creation account has an inescapably liturgical, poetic feel, full of repetition, as if it were intended to be recited. In Genesis 2, the creation of Adam account not only proposes a different order to the creative process (although, to be fair, there is ongoing theological debate about whether that is actually the case and if so, why), it also reads much more as prose than poetry, much more as story than liturgy, to be listened to and taken on board, not recited and claimed as doctrine. This trend continues, with occasional switches in language and theme.

When it comes to source material, the most dominant scholarly conclusion is that all of the various ancient Genesis manuscripts which survive can be separated into two authors, commonly known as the Yahwist (J) source and the Priestly (P) source.

The Yahwist source is so named because of its continual use of God's name Yahweh, and is primarily concerned with telling the history of God's story, but there is no way of identifying a specific author or group of authors, except that the style of writing suggests it was written some time in and around the Babylonian exile.

The Priestly source is so named because of its focus on God's establishment of priesthood and priestly life, but also includes much that links together key elements of prose, often with liturgy or genealogies, and very often with a priority on showing God's sense of order - that amid the uncertainties of the world, including uncertainties about God himself, he has a plan. The P source appears to have been written sometime later than the J source, towards the end of the exilic period, adding to it and joining it together. Again, there is no way of identifying an author or authors, although the date has naturally led to speculation that Ezra may have been directly involved as he was both a prominent priest (perhaps even a high priest) and a champion of God's Torah.

In this understanding, Genesis 1 was written by the Priestly source, whilst the Genesis 2 creation account, and the Eden story that follows, were written by the Yahwist.

Now it can be tempting to find this suggestion of multiple authors offensive, because it seems to fly in the face of what we have always "known." But really, it is only tradition that has ever held that Moses is the sole author, and it really need not be something to worry about if that tradition turns out to be wrong. It in no way compromises the principle that these are God's words.

THE GOD OF PAGE ONE

We are actually very familiar with the concept of God's one final complete Word being scripted by many authors. It is one of the most beautiful aspects of Scripture - the most extraordinary partnership between God and humanity, our relationship expressing itself in power and praise, as God spoke through fallen people to deliver his perfect divine word.

And so we can rest on the promise that The Bible makes of itself: that all scripture is God-breathed, and that it is living and active. God is both the editor-in-chief and the grand narrator, telling his story through the stories of many.

Nonetheless, it is important to acknowledge the different human authors because it taps into how God says different things in different ways to different people at different times, drawing attention to different aspects of his character and his story.

So when it comes to creation, realising that God spoke through two authors can liberate us from the worries about their inconsistency, because it releases us into the understanding that God was merely drawing attention to different aspects of creation. They both tell the truth, from different angles.

Where Genesis 1 largely focuses on revealing God, Genesis 2 largely focuses on revealing humanity, though both naturally shed essential light on each of them. But at the same time, these two passages remain inextricably linked, placed one next to the other, inevitably and deliberately feeding into one another, because God spoke them both into being. Even in their apparent inconsistencies, they share the same message and contribute to our One God telling his one story.

So, as we proceed to read the Priestly source's words in Genesis 1, we can do so in the confidence that this is God's story, told by God, as he seeks to bring specific and significant revelation on the first page of his much bigger story. And so in that confidence, let us open Gods Word to page one and listen to God's voice.

THE GOD OF PAGE ONE

3

THE
GOD
OF
PAGE
ONE

For who is God, but the LORD? And who is a rock, except our God?

Psalm 18 v 31

THE BIBLE begins, very simply, with an introduction. This is a book all about God. It is His story. It is a story that has shaped the world, defined cultures, set standards, changed nations and individuals.

It is a story with a cast of thousands, but ultimately it is all about the One who makes it all happen. This is God's story, so meet God. This is what He is like. This is what He does. This is who made you and everything around you.

Do you want to hear His story?

In chapter one I talked about how we tend to be very quick to search The Bible for answers to the 'when' and 'how' questions, rather than the 'who' and 'why.' I wonder if there is any part of The Bible that has been victim to this approach more than page one.

I have lost count of the number of times I have been asked whether I think this is a literal account or not. Christians and non-Christians alike ask me, sometimes out of genuine open interest, but I suspect more often to ascertain whether I am 'the right sort of Christian.'

I'm not quite sure what 'the right sort of Christian' is exactly, but I'm pretty sure that I don't qualify! For some, it seems to be a measure of how rational a person is ("You're not one of those fundamentalist whackos are you?!"); for others it might be a measure of faith ("You do trust God's Word in the face of so-called evidence, don't you?"). There always seems to be an agenda behind the question and the agenda so often seems to be about checking spiritual credentials: is he a sound theologian, is he in touch with the real world, does he live by faith?

Perhaps you have had a similar experience. Or perhaps you are the one who asks the question of others. I should make it clear, by the way, that I have been that person many times in the past. I have fervently engaged in the debate - and provoked it - believing it to be of vital importance to the foundations of faith. Please do not hear this as a criticism of that, but rather as an invitation to approach the issue from a different perspective.

You see, my observation from my own experience is that the more I pursued this debate, the more 'stiff-necked' I became. This is a phrase that God used to describe the Israelites in the days of the exodus.[11] They had a tendency not to look up to Him, but only to themselves, their needs and wants and the people

---

[11] See Exodus 32 v9, 33 v3, 33 v5, 34 v9.

around them, and this is what I found myself doing when wrestling with others about creation.

However we might interpret Scripture, the measure we should all be able to apply is whether it draws us towards or away from God, and personally I found myself looking more at myself and others when I considered this opening passage. I used my interpretation to forge distinctions between myself and other people, to measure myself against them, and the consequence was this passage became very one dimensional - as if it was written solely to measure the difference between the faithful and the faithless.

And it's not only me. When I have shared this observation with others, people have repeatedly told me they feel exactly the same way, sometimes to the point of feeling unwilling to approach this passage at all because of the controversy that surrounds it. They see areas of conflict, with others and within themselves, as they try and reconcile a passage so at odds with the overwhelming message of the world, and it is a whole lot easier to pretend it isn't there.

This all sounds very one-sided or disapproving, but I don't want to tar everyone with the same brush or to suggest that these things are not important. There are many people who dig in to the literal, the figurative and the liturgical nature of this passage and it certainly does draw them and those they influence closer to their Heavenly Father. Indeed, as Hub Director for Westminster Theological Centre in East Anglia, I have been extremely privileged to work alongside wonderful theologians such as Crispin Fletcher-Louis, Bob Ekblad, Peter Fitch and others, who study and teach these issues head-on in great depth and have unearthed truly amazing revelations about God, about man and about their relationship. What they teach is, I believe, nothing short of life-changing and is always a blessing to me and everyone they share it with.

So clearly there is a huge value - which I have seen transform the spiritual lives of our students here in East Anglia - but it does tend to take a considerable amount of time for study, money for course fees, access to relevant material and access to good teaching before that value is usually discovered, and on the whole this contains the treasure within the keep of the academic theological world. The majority only have the words of Genesis to go on, according to the translation they happen to own, as well as the context in which they have heard this passage addressed before.

Very sadly, therefore, in all honesty I would say my aforementioned colleagues and students are the exception and that the same did not apply in most cases I have encountered. And for me, outside of the world of dedicated theological study, it certainly encouraged my stiff neck and drew my eyes away from God, towards myself.

Furthermore, the more I thought about it, the stranger it seemed to me that the opening words of The Bible would be so divisive. Surely there are higher priorities at this stage? So, I began to seek a different approach. Of course, the debate didn't go away, and it continues to be one of the most common topics I am asked about.

Usually, the question centres on evolution, and very often it comes out of nowhere: "So, Freddy, which do you think is true: creation or evolution?" Just occasionally it might centre more on the age of the earth and the universe. "So, Freddy, what about that big bang, then?"

The reason I say that I don't qualify as 'the right sort of Christian' in these scenarios is that when I am asked this question, my response is always one of disinterest, albeit hopefully a friendly one. To an extent, I suppose this is because I'm not keen on being surveyed for my credibility - this may be a niggle of pride kicking in - but really I am not interested in the answer at all. I realise this will make some of you reading this uncomfortable - please bear with me if it does! - but I have to say I'm not at all bothered whether Genesis 1 is literal or not.

My reasoning is simple and threefold. First, I don't actually think this is what the passage is addressing. We will come back to this more in a moment, but for now let me leave it at the observation that it is surely clear that whoever wrote the book, as well as everyone who read it and lived by it at the time, had no intentions of trying to tackle this debate.

We are talking about an account from many thousands of years before evolution and the Big Bang were first conceived and many generations before science was seen as a viable (or even necessary) way of explaining our existence or our place in the universe. Genesis 1 in no way reads as a scientific document, so it seems terribly unfair to judge it as one and against others. I appreciate this is over-simplifying the issue, but as I say, we will return to this shortly.

Second, I am liable to be wrong. Even if I were educated to the hilt in history, theology, sociology, biology, physics, chemistry, mathematics and literature (which I would need to be to fully understand the depth of both sides of the argument), I am still liable to be wrong since I am a flawed human, with limited intelligence and imagination, a tendency towards being argumentative and prideful of my own opinion, and a strong sense of loyalty to the philosophy I have adopted. I am not putting myself down in any way. This is simply part of the deal of being human and we all wrestle with these things.

It means that I am very aware that even if I were fully furnished with the depths of the arguments, I would still be likely to miss the truth. And in any case, I fall so far short of knowing it all that I really have no leg to stand on in the debate. I will only get shot down immediately by the one person in the room who knows just that little bit more (who always seems to be present!), and the debate goes nowhere.

More importantly, though, I look at the people who do know the depths of their respective perspectives, who have spent their whole lives digging only into this one issue, who are some of the cleverest and wisest theological, scholarly and scientific minds in the world, and they are unable to agree. Indeed, after more than a hundred years research and debate, they only seem to be getting further apart - often based on the same evidence!

And it's not like it's simply a matter of the theologians versus the scientists. On the contrary, one scientist will state boldly that all the evidence points to evolution, big bang and a universe governed by the determination of physics. Another scientist will state equally as boldly that the same evidence points to intelligent design and the impossibility of evolution.

One theologian will assure us that Genesis 1 describes an exact and literal account of the creation of the earth and universe, and will prove it by pointing to all the places in the Bible and to the archaeological evidence about how the world thought and lived at the time that supports his conclusion. Another theologian will point to all the same evidence to assure us that Genesis 1 is liturgical, or poetic, or giving a sense of the order of what happened rather than a primitive photograph.

If these eminent people cannot agree, then I am not going to get any closer to it than them. To be honest, it suggests to me that at a fundamental level the wrong questions are being asked, but again, more on that in a moment.

Third, my place in heaven is not dependent on whether I get this right. Last time I checked, I was not expecting a multiple choice exam upon entry into the Kingdom:

"Well, Freddy, you have done very well so far, you've ticked A for *Jesus died for you*, and C for *Read The Bible to hear God's words*, now for the biggie ... Oh, I am sorry, you got that one wrong. Next please."

I realise I am being flippant, but it does feel like we can raise the importance of this passage to the level of a salvation-breaker, and it simply isn't.

I'm not suggesting for one moment that we don't get closer to God by engaging with this passage - indeed, as we will come to shortly, I am suggesting that this passage is critical for properly understanding and deepening our relationship with God - but I *am* suggesting that if we come to God with an open heart, humble, repentant and relying on the cross, looking to Jesus, expectant of the Holy Spirit, spending time in relationship with God, then not knowing if this passage is literal or not is not going to have an impact on our heavenly reservation.

I know many Spirit-filled, faithful and fruitful Christians who fall on both sides of this particular "literal-or-not" fence and my only conclusion must be that the presence and power of God is not determined by a literal or otherwise acceptance of creation, but on our relationship with and worship of the creator, our loving Father God.

It comes back to what I said in chapter one. The important questions are not 'when' and 'how' but 'who' and 'why'. If we ask when creation happened, or how it happened, then we find no clear cut answers. Indeed, the Bible is sufficiently vague that the most eminent theologians do not agree. But if we ask who created and why did He do it, then suddenly we find we have a wealth of very specific answers. If we take the activity of creation away from the centre-stage and make the creator the focus, the whole passage opens up.

And so we come full circle. The Bible is God's story and His story begins, not with a scientific explanation of the start of the universe, but with an introduction. Meet God. This is what He is like. We know this because we watch what He does.

Genesis, the same as the rest of The Bible, was written by people who knew nothing of evolution, nothing of the big bang, and little of scientific discovery. But they knew God. They had no interest in defending the precision of creation, no agenda to uphold or debunk scientific endeavour. All that was in their sights was to reveal who God is, who we are and how we can relate. Their story is His story. And it begins by introducing who He is.

This is not a passage that is the exclusive property of confirmed academics, or of those with a point to make. This is a passage that should set the tone of faith for all of us. Here is our God, revealing Himself to us for the first time, showing us everything we need to understand about Him for the rest of His Word to make sense.

By the end of this account we will already know Him intimately, so that everything we see Him doing throughout Scripture - and continue to see Him doing in our lives and in the world around us - will make sense if we get to know the God of page one. This is a passage for all, and can set us on the road to an engaging relationship with God.

So, let's meet God. For the next few chapters we are going to examine the seven days of creation in close detail. And as we do, there is one question I want us to ask above all others: what does this tell us about who God is?

Let us begin at the beginning ...

4

IN
THE
BEGINNING

In the beginning God created the heavens and the earth.

Genesis 1 v 1

64

STUDY QUESTIONS (1)

Read Genesis 1 v 1-2.

What does God's presence "in the beginning" tell us about Him?

What does the description of this primeval earth evoke in your mind? Have you ever experienced anything that might be called dark, formless or void?

Where is God in these dark, formless or void times?

Key question: What does it tell us about God that He "was hovering over the face of the waters?"

NOTES

IN THE BEGINNING

IT MAY be that the opening two verses of Genesis form the start of the first day but I have to say I have never read it that way. It seems clear to me that the pattern that is established is that each day begins with the words, "And God said."

Read this way, these opening verses act as the introduction, which gives us a tantalising glimpse into what we are about to discover. Verse one might better end with a colon rather than a full-stop, because everything that follows relates back to this first statement.

"In the beginning God created the heavens and the earth: and this is how it happened."

And then verse two sets the scene.

It is a wonderful story-telling technique and at its heart, this is what Genesis 1 is doing: revealing who God is by telling His first and greatest story.

You want to know about who God is?

Well ...

67

THE GOD OF PAGE ONE

*In the beginning God created the heavens and
the earth. The earth was without form and void,
and darkness was over the face of the deep.
And the Spirit of God was hovering
over the face of the waters.*

Genesis 1 v 1-2

The setting is clear, it is dramatic, and God is right at the centre of it. Despite this dark and brooding opening, we are left in no doubt that this is God's story. He is the focus, the one around whom all the drama unfolds. And the drama is epic in its proportions.

I can imagine the first people hearing this story looking into the night sky as they listened and being amazed: God is bigger than all of this.

God made all of this.

God is connected to all of this.

Wow.

Already this is a story worth hearing.

We read on, as a child, restless in anticipation of what we are about to hear.

But these opening words are so much more than a mere introduction. They are words of significant revelation, which display fundamental truths about God which are unpacked in finer detail in the account that follows.

To really grapple with them, let's zoom in and look at this one statement at a time.

IN THE BEGINNING

In the beginning God created the
heavens and the earth.

Genesis 1 v 1

Within three words of the Bible starting we know something amazing about God. God precedes the beginning. There is no date offered for when the beginning was, because that is not what matters here. What matters is that at the point of beginning - the initiation of space and time - God was already there.

God is the creator not only of space but time as well. One of the scientific discoveries of the last century that astonishes me most is the understanding of time not as a universally consistent measurement but as a distinct part of the fabric of the universe, which is bent and shaped by the forces within the universe, chiefly the effect exerted by mass.[12]

Here, it seems to me, we find scientists and the author of Genesis 1 singing from the same hymn sheet, so to speak. The Bible agrees that time is part of the fabric of the universe (or "heavens" as most translations call it), since time is initiated at the point

---

[12] This 'geodetic effect' was first asserted by Albert Einstein in his Theory of General Relativity (1916, republished in Albert Einstein, *Relativity: The Special and the General Theory*, Pober Publishing Co, 2010), but has only been 'proven' to the satisfaction of the majority scientific world in the last few years. One such proof is detailed in the Gravity Probe B project, as described in the paper *Gravity Probe B: Final Results of a Space Experiment to Test General Relativity*, Physical Review Letters, 2011).

of the creation of the universe, denoted by the phrase "in the beginning" - a statement of measured time.

Clearly something must have preceded the universe, because God was already there, but whatever existed, it was not measurable by time. Science and The Bible can find happy agreement here. They only disagree about the intention.

Currently, the scientific world's most accepted explanation is that space and time are the result essentially of pressure (i.e. the Big Bang).[13] The Bible tells us that space and time were intentional, and preceding all of it is God. He is therefore not subject to time and space, He exists outside of it and yet, as we see in verse two, He is able to enter into it. Time and space are subject to Him. He can bend and shape it just as gravity can, and it cannot apply its own influences - those of change and decay - over Him.

This brings us two extraordinary revelations: God is eternal and God is powerful.

Let's look first at our eternal God. He looks over time from the outside. He is able to see across the span of history from the beginning of creation to the end, and therefore neither the beginning nor the end can have any hold over Him. God has no beginning and no end, and right from the start of our relationship with Him we can hold this close to our hearts and minds.

---

[13] This is described in detail throughout Stephen Hawking's *A Brief History of Time* (Bantam, 1995), but probably most accessibly discussed in chapter 8: 'The Origin and Fate of the Universe.'

If God speaks into the future, He speaks with authority because He can see it. If He invites us to live by His side in eternity, His invitation has credibility because His dwelling place never perishes and He is able to span the distance between His eternal Kingdom and this temporary creation (v2).

He does not change,[14] because He is not subject to the forces that compel change. He does not diminish, He does not falter, He does not cease to be there.

There are more than 750,000 words in any given English translation of the Bible. We know all this after only three.

And then as we read on we see His power, and the more that is discovered about the heavens and the earth the more this power only seems to magnify. God created everything. There is nothing in all of creation that can equal His power and might because everything is subject to Him and is only as strong as He has made them.

Even at the time this must have been an awesome statement. Now, when we know so much more about universe, such as the unbelievable power that is generated by our sun alone, which is only a medium-sized star, let alone the real solar giants or even the devastating power of a black hole, our view of God's power becomes so awesome that it is impossible to get a hold of.

---

[14] Hebrews 13 v8

We know there is no limit to His might just as there is no limit to His lifespan. And we are still only ten words in! So, what of the second statement?

The earth was without form and void, and darkness was over the face of the deep.
And the Spirit of God was hovering over the face of the waters.

Genesis 1 v 2

God is always there. He is present even in the formless and dark places. And how is He there? He is there intimately, close, hovering over His creation. This goes beyond necessity and is more than affection; this is passion, adoration, the deepest of connections. This is God showing how completely in love with His creation He is.

Even before it has any shape, any distinction or sign of goodness, He stays close. All He wants is to be connected, to spend time, as close as He can to his beloved, even in the darkness and the void. And so He hovers over the waters. There is almost the feel of Him lingering, unable to draw Himself away, fascinated by how wonderful it already is. God's love is so tangible.

It is also a love that is not based in any way on achievement or having earned it. Creation has not yet had the chance to reciprocate God's love, nor contribute to His plan. It hasn't even got a form. There is nothing good yet to be said of creation

72

except that it is the handiwork of God and because of that, He loves it with passionate urgency.

God's passionate love for His creation is established before creation even really gets going. He loves creation because of what it is, not what it does. As the listener to this story we are compelled to think: how much more does He love us for who *we* are and not what *we* do?

These are the three fundamental characteristics of God: that He is eternal, He is powerful and He is loving. If we know these things, then not only will everything else that follows make sense, but even if you strip all of that away, you are still left with a glorious and full revelation of who God is and why we should find him awesome, fascinating and our most treasured companion.

Thousands of years later, when Paul was describing what really mattered in a Christian life to the church in Corinth, he identified three things that remained when all else was gone. They were faith, hope and love, with love being the greatest.[15] Faith draws us to live in God's strength, according to His power; hope draws us to wait on a life with God in eternity; love connects us to the heartbeat of God, and it is the greatest because where faith and hope draw our lives closer to God, when we love, we are actually sharing God's experience, and we are experiencing who God is. His power and timelessness are glorious because of His love.

---

[15] 1 Corinthians 13 v13

The opening paragraph of Genesis gives us such an amazing revelation of God, and really it tells us everything. If the author of Genesis had not written anything else, if the whole Bible had not got beyond its first two verses, we would still know God as eternal, powerful and loving, and so we would know enough to worship Him, serve Him, love Him and relate with Him.

Everything that follows serves to give greater clarity to these first three revelations. Therefore, for the rest of this creation account - indeed, for the rest of The Bible - to really take hold of us we need only to have grasped these three foundational truths, because we see all three of these at work in everything that now unfolds. So let us read on, meeting God afresh, with these in mind. And let us see how much more of Him we discover.

5

THE
FIRST
DAY

And God said, "Let there be light,"
and there was light.

Genesis 1 v 3

STUDY QUESTIONS (2)

Read Genesis 1 v 3-5.

What does it say about God that He calls light into being, rather than fashions it with His own hands?

What makes the light good?

Key question: Why does God choose to separate light and darkness, and give each its own space, rather than getting rid of darkness altogether?

Is there any significance that Jesus is identified as the Light of the World?

NOTES

WE HAVE already seen how God is powerful and loves His creation, and now we see that access to both of these is through His words as God speaks creation into being:

And God said, "Let there be light," and there was light. And God saw that the light was good. And God separated the light from the darkness. God called the light Day, and the darkness he called Night. And there was evening and there was morning, the first day.

Genesis 1 v 3-5

The first day initiates a pattern of how God creates that repeats throughout the seven days. It is a simple progression that sets up how He interacts with His creation, and as we follow it, so much of God's character is revealed: First, He calls into being. Second, He ascribes value. Third, He separates. Fourth, He names.

So what is revealed on this day? Let's look at the first step: calling into being. Having established that God is loving, powerful and eternal, we now see that the way into these characteristics is through His voice. His voice expresses His power, His voice expresses His character, His voice expresses His heart. If we want to get to know God, if we want to see him at work, if we want to have a relationship with Him, we must listen to His voice.

Already we should be in no doubt that what God wants is a relationship. We see here that God is a God of relationship, who includes that which He creates in doing His work and sharing in His life. God could have formed light by His own hands, He could have done it silently, He could have remained distant, but He didn't. Instead, He invited creation into this activity.

He called out for light to be, and it was. Call and response. He told creation how to respond - "Let there be light," and there was light. He did not fashion light or, as we shall see in the following days, seas or land or plants out of nothing with His hands; He invited creation to produce light and creation responded.

Here we have the first tangible example of a relationship at work. God invited creation into a new form and creation responded because it knew God's voice, the source of His eternal will, His power and His love. The universe is founded on a relationship and the first day places the importance of that relationship at the very heart of God's plan.

This is reinforced further on the sixth day, in verse 26, when God says, "Let us make man ..." We will come to the full significance of this in due time, but for the moment let us settle for observing the use of the word "us." Relationship is at the heart of God's plan because relationship is at the heart of His character and His identity. These are pre-Trinitarian days, in that God has yet to reveal Himself as the Trinity, and yet His language reveals the community He shares within Himself.

Indeed, the word 'God' alone is a significant enough clue, at least it would have been to the first hearers of this account. The word in Hebrew is 'elohiym,' which although we translate as singular God, is in fact a pluralised word.

The singular form of this is 'elowahh' and tends only to be used when describing God in impersonal terms, and it doesn't feature anywhere in Genesis. In fact, the place we find this word the most is in Job, where God is repeatedly referred to by those who do not know Him. But throughout The Bible, those who do know Him know Him as elohiym, the God of community who is a community, and so communes with Himself. This quality of His character will become incredibly important later in the creative process.

When considering how God's plurality is revealed in Genesis 1, you may even want to go further than this. You may agree with me that, although far from explicit, here is the first time we in fact can see God present in all His Trinity, with each distinctly identifiable.

We have already had the fatherly expression of God present in the beginning (which we will see more clearly a little later) and the Spirit of God hovering over the waters. Now we have the word and light of God, both of which are familiar identifications of Jesus.

Jesus identifies himself as light[16] and John opens his book by identifying Jesus as the Word of God.[17] Of course, John also says that Jesus was present at creation[18] and we might also see Jesus' words, "Before Abraham was born, I am!"[19] as being another pointer to his presence as early as the first day.

On this basis, I don't believe it is too much of a stretch to look for him there, nor to find him. Personally I find this one of those joys that the hindsight afforded by the New Testament brings.

It's like watching the move *The Usual Suspects,* which is a great movie as you watch it but it is only when it ends that you realise there was so much more you could have seen. So you go back and watch it again and the experience is completely different as you spot so much more that had always been there but you hadn't initially known enough to recognise.

---

[16] John 8 v12
[17] John 1 v1
[18] John 1 v3
[19] John 8 v58

All that being said, it is safe to say that the original hearers of this story would not have seen a Trinitarian God here, but in light of the cross, I believe Jesus is there for us to see. But even if we stop short of so bold a claim, it remains clear that we have a God of relationship being displayed throughout the seven days, revealed through His identity and His calling out to creation, starting from day one.

Having called out, He then ascribes value to what emerges. He saw that it was good. It is so simple a turn of phrase and yet so powerful. The goodness described is pure, without need of qualification. It is without blemish, it is beautiful. In every way it could be, very simply and very powerfully, it is good.

And what makes it good? For one thing, it is good because God recognises that it is. This is a principle that we need to grasp right from the beginning. Things are good if God sees them as such. We cannot look at ourselves or others or situations and judge the goodness of them as well as He can.

If God looks at you and says you are good (which, by the way, He does!), then you are. If God looks at light and says that it is good, then it is. And if something is good, then it has a place in God's handiwork.

For another, the only specific influence we might identify as a reason for things being good is the relationship we have already seen, since this is the one thing to have taken place as a measure for the light's goodness. God wants a relationship, in which

He includes His creation in His work as well as His rest (as we shall see in chapter eleven: the seventh day), and every time He sees it happening He is delighted and sees that it is good. This, too, is such an encouragement. God calls out and all who respond are good in His eyes.

This moment also builds into creation perhaps the most fundamental instinct that all created living things share: to pursue the light. It is an understanding that is built deep within us. Light equals life. Light is the best we can have. Light is good.

With our New Testament hindsight in place we make the immediate link that Jesus is the light of the world and so Jesus equals life, Jesus is the best we can have, Jesus is what we pursue, and Jesus is good. But even before the New Testament, the significance of light would not have been lost.

So what is it about light, and what does it tell us about God that He recognises it as good? First, and most simple, it enables us to see. Light itself is invisible. It sounds ridiculous to say it, but it stands to reason. If light were visible then all we would ever see would be a blanket of whiteness. In fact, light is invisible until it hits something, and only then does it show itself - or rather, it shows what it has hit. Light exists only to reveal other things.

God is a revealer. He could see His creation without the need of light - He was able to hover over the waters even in total darkness - but He wants us to be able to see His creation too, to be able to share it and search its depths. God takes joy in what He has made and He wants us to experience that same joy.

I'm pretty sure He isn't angry with people who devote their lives to science and reason, because they are using their eyes and minds to see what He has made. He must be so devastated that so many of them are making that journey outside of a relationship with Him, not only because they tend to miss the full glory of what He has done because they do not recognise Him in it, but also because He loves them deeply and would love to be the one taking them on the tour. These are people He has gifted with the ability to search creation's roots - how much joy would God take to be talking them through it all as they discover more and more.

But I digress! Even for the majority of us who are not gifted in that direction, being able to see God's creation is one of the greatest joys available to us, and so often the ultimate evidence of God's existence and handiwork. This is called the numinous effect: to be in awe of creation and see God at work.

But we might see more than this being described, because in the vivid picture of creation that is being painted - don't worry whether it is literal or not for the moment, just picture the scene - it is not only creation that can be seen, but God also. God can see in the darkness, but we cannot and He intends Himself to be seen, and to be found in the light. God is a revealer and He is also a revelation.

For a God who wants a relationship with us, our ability to see is critical. Without light we are stripped of our best way of seeing Him. Without light we are stripped of our best way of seeing His handiwork. Without light we are stripped of our best way of seeing one another.

Light is also the way we are able to navigate creation. We will look at this more closely when we examine the fourth day, but it is clear even from day one that God wants us to do this. We are not to stand still. It is the first hint we have that God will not stand still, but is a God on the move ... but it is only a hint.

And light is also good because, as we will come to see in the days that follow, it is a critical building block in His plan to create life. Indeed, for all the life that is described in Genesis 1, both light and water are essential, and both are in place by the first day.

Of course, it may be that most people hearing the first telling of this account would not be aware of light and water's significance in the race for life. Nevertheless, anyone hearing this story at the time would already know that this was a great story, and that God was the author, so He is a story-teller. They would therefore already be aware that this day was taking the story somewhere and light was in some way crucial to the plot.

The opening verses alone ought to be enough to tell us that God has a plan, but if not then we can certainly see it now. God is building towards something and every building block towards it is good.

The third step I identified God taking on each day of creation is that He separates. It seems to be a consistent pattern that creating something always involves separation. That is not to say that separation is a bad thing - indeed, in almost every instance in Genesis 1 the separation is described as a good thing, necessary even, for creation to adopt the variety God has planned for it.

In this case we see the separation of the light from the darkness. As it happens, this seems to be another example of the biblical description bearing close resemblance to the scientific understanding of light, since although we now define darkness in terms of an absence of light, darkness must have preceded light since light is a physical entity in the form of photons, which at some point - be it literal Genesis creation or the Big Bang - emerged into being to create light. In other words, because of light's absence, darkness preceded light.

Again, the key distinction here lies in the intention. There was no accident in creation, and God speaks light into being on purpose. It is the first thing He creates - in all of creation it is the most fundamental[20], it is His top priority.

Darkness is never identified as being synonymous with badness but this passage goes to such lengths to

---

[20] This is interesting given that light - particularly its speed - is the one recognised constant in creation.

identify the things that are good that the compelling conclusion is that anything not called good must be bad. This being the case, on day one we see a God who looks for light in the darkness. And we know that we have a God who is able to find it. He can look into the dark places and draw out the light and if it is not there, He can call it into being.

God understands the distinction between light and darkness, and He invites us to live in the light, but He does not offer us a world without darkness. There is no banishing of darkness - light will always overrule darkness and yet God still makes space for it. However, as we have already seen in verse two, God is present in the darkness.

How important a revelation this is for humanity! We have a God who can still see us when we are in dark places in our lives, and when He finds us He is looking for the light, and is able to call it into being if necessary. Even in our darkest days - whether our darkness is spiritual, emotional, physical, mental, or whatever - He is there with us, and as long as we hold on to Him, His light will overrule the darkness that surrounds us.

And just imagine how it must have felt for the original hearers of this account, who lived in a much harsher world than the one most of us now enjoy, surrounded by danger, especially during the night, which was so much darker and threatening than most of us now experience. Imagine how it must have felt to know that God was there, hovering over them, able to protect them and ready to call light into the darkness. How could they have ever forgotten God's love for them, His power and His ever-presence? [21]

The last step in God's daily pattern is that He names what He has made. This is the first time he names what He creates; it is an honour He continues throughout the seven days and it tells us yet another characteristic of God - he is a God who confers identity.

The identity that He gives to light is Day - the time when life is lived to its fullest, the time when work is done, the time of fruitfulness. With this identity comes purpose. God sees the light for what it is and sees that it is good and on that basis confers a purpose upon it - to reveal, to guide, to enable life to move and grow - because these are the things God does and wants His creation to do also. And yet at this time there is nothing for light to influence. God gives identity and purpose before any work is called for. It is based simply on His assertion that it is good.

How much more can the same be said of us? How much more would those who heard this account in those early days have understood that their God was a God who called them into being, looked upon them and saw that they were good, and on that basis alone

---

[21] Probably the best I have ever heard this both taught and applied comes from Bob Ekblad, who tells some amazing stories about how this side of God's nature has transformed the lives of prisoners and gang members in Seattle, USA. For more of this, a highly recommended read is his book *Reading the Bible with the Damed* (John Knox Press, 2005).

gave them an identity and a purpose before they had any work to do; and all this not because of who they were but because of who God is.

And one last quick observation: here is the moment that time begins to take hold. Here we have the first evening, the first morning. The God that preceded time now initiates it and reigns over it.

So to summarise, by the end of the first day we know that God is eternal, He is powerful, He is loving, He is relational, He invites those in relationship with Him into His work, He is a story-teller, He has a plan, He wants us to see and share and delight in His creation, He draws light from the dark places but is still present in the darkness, He reveals and is a revelation, He is a guide, He gives identity and purpose.

We already know so much about God but we will rewrite this list at the end of our exploration of the seven days and see how much more we know of our God from page one.

6

THE
SECOND
DAY

*And God said, "Let there be an expanse
in the midst of the waters ..."*

Genesis 1 v 6

STUDY QUESTIONS (3)

Read Genesis 1 v 6-8.

How would you describe creation before the expanse is made?

Why did there need to be an expanse, and what happened to God in this moment?

What does it tell us about God that He made the expanse, rather than called it into being?

Key question: Why does God not call the second day good?

NOTES

I HAVE highlighted where I think we can see the first day establishing a pattern of behaviour that God follows for the rest of creation: that He calls, He affirms, He separates and He names. These can be identified as clearly in the second day as in any other, but for us to really get to grips with the significance of this day, we will need to address all four of these in one go:

> *And God said, "Let there be an expanse*
> *in the midst of the waters, and let it*
> *separate the waters from the waters."*
> *And God made the expanse and separated*
> *the waters that were under the expanse*
> *from the waters that were above the*
> *expanse. And it was so. And God called the*
> *expanse Heaven. And there was evening and there*
> *was morning, the second day.*

Genesis 1 v 6-8

The second day is a day of massive significance for the whole of creation and, indeed, the whole of God's plan. The separation we are talking about is not the separation of the waters on earth into oceans - that happens on the third day. These are the waters that make up the primary substance of creation. In the opening verses of Genesis we are introduced to a world that is characterised only by water. Here we have the next clear sign of a process going on.

This is the day where we really get the first insights into where God's plan is leading and yet because it is still such early days, and because we do not have God's perspective, it is all too easy for us to miss the goodness of what happens.

What God calls into being here is quite hard to comprehend until we understand that the ancient Hebrews considered the universe - or 'heaven'[22] as verse eight puts it - to be a physical, limited space with solid edges. We can see this from the word that was used to describe it. In the English Standard Version (ESV) it is 'expanse,' which seems a fair description of how we now see the universe. But the Hebrew word is 'rakeah,' which literally means "an extended, solid surface."[23] Many historians and

---

[22] The Hebrew word here is 'shamayim', which literally means 'to be lofty' and is the Hebrew word for the sky, including the 'higher ether where the celestial bodies revolve' - i.e. the universe. See James Strong, *Strong's Hebrew Dictionary of the Bible*, Miklal Software Solutions, 2011, H8064.

[23] James Strong, *Strong's Hebrew Dictionary of the Bible*, Miklal Software Solutions, 2011, H7549.

theologians also agree that this was not a figurative use of language, but that this was the common view held in the Ancient Near East.[24]

We also need to keep in mind what the scene looks like at the start of this day. The Spirit of God has not withdrawn during the first day so continues to hover over the waters. However, now these waters separate so that, although the Spirit of God continues to hover, those waters over which He hovers are lifted above the solid entity of the heavens, leaving the waters of the earth below. This is the moment that God is separated from His creation.

The significance of this in God's mind can be seen by the observation that this is the only day in creation that God does not look at and acknowledge as good. It is the only day where God's appraisal of His work is not affirming. To reinforce this, we might also consider what must have happened to the light at this moment.

We have already established that light is invisible, but that it reveals everything it touches. So when light is called into being it reveals the waters - at this point the entirety of creation in one place. However, when the waters are separated the expanse is

---

[24] For example, see G. K. Beale's *The Erosion of Inerrancy in Evangelicalism: Responding to the New Challenges to Biblical Authority*, pp.197-198, Crossway, 2008; also in P. H. Seely's article 'The Firmament and the Water Above' from *The Westminster Theological Journal 53*, 1991; and also 'The Three-Storey Universe' from N. F. Gier's *God, Reason, and the Evangelicals*, chapter 13, University Press of America, 1987.

virtually empty. Certainly light can reveal the Earth but what of the rest of the heavens? They were lit up on the first day but they must return to darkness on the second, for in the vastness of the universe, before the ignition of the stars, there is nothing for the light to reveal. The onset of darkness in this picture only adds to the sense that what had at first seemed so good, suddenly falls into question.

But surely all of God's work in creation is good? After all, in only a few paragraphs time we read about how God looked at His completed work at the end of the sixth day and saw that it was all very good, which must certainly include the work of the second day. So on the face of it, it seems we have a contradiction: how can God not see this day as good, whilst everything He does is good?

The key to unlocking this riddle is to put ourselves in God's place for a moment. God is passionate about the heavens and the earth. He cannot draw Himself away. He hovers over them as a doting parent does their newborn child. He is also a God of relationship, who intimately interacts with and involves creation in His work. But He also has a plan, and for this plan to work it is necessary for Him to withdraw.

It is only on the sixth day that we can see the plan with any level of clarity. I don't want to put in too much of a spoiler now but I imagine this passage is familiar enough for us to know that God's plan involves humanity ruling over creation - something we cannot do if God is also there. There can be no king over Him, after all.

THE SECOND DAY

We will see that what God is building towards is a plan that continues to see Him actively involved with His creation, and physically present in His creation, but being so *through* humanity. His plan is to elevate us above the rest of creation so that we can share in the most intimate relationship with Him, and share also in His work in creation.

But for all of this to work He must become separated from His creation. He must be absent before the first life appears on earth, so that the only physical ruler life ever knows is humanity.

This is an unavoidable moment if this plan is to be fulfilled, and in the wider perspective of God's plan - which He sees and we do not see - this is the best of the good news days. But it is no wonder that God does not look on this day as a good day - the day He is separated from his beloved baby.

We see so much of God in this moment, but we do have to take it all in one go. If we were to look at what He says, followed by how He affirms, followed by how He separates, followed by how He names, then we might fool ourselves into thinking this is a bad day. We might also fool ourselves into seeing a God who distances Himself, who keeps Himself isolated and aloof, who is impersonal, callous even, as He leave's creation's side before bringing life into the world.

If we want to see it, we can see God creating a physical barrier between Him and creation, as if He felt the need to be elevated above us, holy in His unattainability, further beyond our touch than we could ever reach, and yet we have already seen how passionately He loves His creation.

It seems to me that it is already impossible to see God in this way if we have paid attention to the first day. God has already revealed Himself to be loving, relational and inclusive - He is hardly going to turn His back on that with His very next action. I sometimes wonder if there aren't people whose view of God is compromised simply because they didn't engage with Him until the second day.

Certainly the reader is invited to feel the lack of 'goodness' on this day, but it is not to distance God in our mind, rather to draw us closer, to pay attention to how God is shaping creation. The drama of the story is unavoidable. I can almost hear the childlike reaction of the first listeners, who heard that the waters were separated and watched in their mind as God's Spirit was lifted away from the earth: "Why must he be separated?" It seems at this stage that it must be very bad news.

In fact, we find out in a few verses that this is actually the first step in setting up an even more powerful and intimate relationship between God and man. We discover that this is about God elevating us, not Himself - elevating us above the rest of creation. We are given access to God that nothing else gets, and with hindsight we see here the first step towards establishing us in His kingly role. But we cannot see it at this point.

At this point we only see how much it hurts God. It is a reminder of how much He loves creation, how much He values it. By the time He gives creation to us, we can be in no doubt how precious a thing it is that He has entrusted us with. But as we read through, we find ourselves wondering what is going on in this moment.

This is the first bit of the story that doesn't seem to fit - something that will happen time and again throughout the Bible, because we don't see things with the same perspective that He does and so we do not understand the mystery of why He does some things.

Do you remember the example from Genesis 22 that I highlighted in chapter one? Sarah had no way of understanding the enormity and the goodness of what God was doing in forcing her to wait so long for a child, because she had no way of seeing with His perspective. She had no way of seeing that God was in the process of elevating her and moving the meta-narrative forwards. To her, it only seemed like bad news, because of her spiritual short-sightedness, when all along it was the very best of news for her and for the rest of history. Well, here is another of those moments.

Here is a moment that is critical to God elevating us, and critical to moving the meta-narrative forwards, but right now it just doesn't seem to fit. It seems out of character, but as we take a step back we see the lengths He is ready to go to in order to share His creation and Himself with us above all others.

When I read this I cannot see the remote God that I have sometimes heard described. It seems to me that if we look at God's four-fold daily pattern - calling, affirming, separating, naming - all in one go, and from the understanding that God is playing a longer game here, then we get a different picture altogether.

We find a God who yearns for intimacy, who isn't satisfied with a relationship of servitude with humanity, as will be the case with the rest of creation, but has a plan to invite us into the intimacy of His presence and the experience of His power. We find a God who is willing to make any sacrifice in order to see this come to pass, including cutting Himself off from His most beloved. Already Jesus' sacrifice is in keeping with God's character. We find a God who is humble, willing to get out of the way in order for us to receive the honour He is due.

We also find a God who creates order out of chaos. We need to pause and dwell on this for a moment, because this is an important and common theological observation about God. In fact, this is such a universally accepted characteristic that it features in almost every ancient religious creation story there is. This is perhaps most significantly true of the Babylonian creation account - the Enuma Elish[25] - which also involves the order of creation being drawn from the chaos of waters.

---

[25] This is reproduced in Leonard William King's *The Seven Tablets of Creation: Enua Elish Complete* (CreateSpace, 2010).

This is often used as an academic argument to dilute the trust-worthiness of Genesis 1: surely we see here that it cannot be trusted, because it is clearly only one example of a much wider form of literature? Or perhaps it is not merely a form of literature, but is actually a political statement? It has been postulated that the Hebrew creation story first emerged written down around the time of the exile at the hands of Babylon, and that therefore this explains the similarity between the two accounts. The argument runs that this is the Hebraic answer to the Enuma Elish, which tells broadly the same story but emphasising that there is only one God.

However, there are several other considerable differences between the two accounts that suggest that this may be an over-simplified conclusion. Perhaps most notably, there is a different starting point and a different purpose. In the Enuma Elish the universe appears already to exist when creation begins. The gods are a part of this creation, and therefore subject to it, although they can exert huge influence over it. The world is then created as a consequence of the battles between the gods.

The purpose of the Babylonian story seems clearly to establish Marduk as the primary god among gods, and to establish humanity as being made to serve the gods.

In Genesis, however, we are presented with a God who creates everything and is subject to nothing; and who creates humanity for the purpose of relationship with Him and to rule over the earth through men and women. We find a personal God, who loves and pays attention to His creation, not a tyrant who demands servitude.

Certainly there are literary similarities, and the accounts appear to follow the same broad progression, but at each stage the Hebrew account makes sure to emphasise the characteristics of God that the Babylonian account misses or undermines.

To me, the Enuma Elish reads far more like Chinese Whispers. It seems to me that in the beginning there was one common creation story, but that as it spread across miles and generations in an oral culture, it was changed and adapted as people drifted further and further from God's presence.[26]

In this understanding, it is no wonder that the basic themes are shared, even if the details can become extraordinarily different! But then, in the absence of an extraordinary God among them, it is also no wonder they have to find other extraordinary explanations.

It would therefore make absolute sense that when the Israelite and Babylonian cultures collided during the exile, that they would be faced with these two creation accounts - one of which has become warped by a lack of ongoing relationship with God, and the Israelites would be eager to set the record straight. It would also explain why they didn't stop at a creation account but went on to piece together the ongoing story of God's relationship with creation and His

---

[26] It is tempting to see the Tower of Babel's influence in this.

people. The Babylonians used gods to justify their culture and lifestyle, to hold them where they were, but the Israelites knew God. They knew He was not a concept to be manipulated, but was real and continued to influence the world in a very real way. They knew that God was on the move, that He was leading them forwards and that His story needed to be told.

However, I am not a scholar of ancient cultures so don't take my word for it. What I would say, though, is that I am fascinated not only by the differences in these creation stories, but also the similarities. These common themes are where we find the core characteristics of God that have survived the edits of history and politics and which have persisted across distance and cultures. And the two features that survive above all others are: first, that He creates powerfully; and second, that He draws order from chaos.

So what is the significance of this? It is a reinforcement of what we already know from before the first day. God is present in the darkness. He is present in the chaos and He knows how to bring it into order.

This is another example where we might look at what scientists have discovered and see their work confirming how Genesis introduces God. We see the universe and it is a space of chaos - with rocks flying through the void, crashing into one another, stars exploding and being born, black holes destroying everything in their reach; and yet we also see a universe, and particularly an Earth, of such precision and complexity, where the planets and the stars move like clockwork and everything on this planet seems to be positioned perfectly for life to thrive.

We look at our perfect blue planet amid the expanse and danger of space and we see what it really means to have drawn order from chaos. Order brings with it sustainability, beauty and life, the promise of which is even clearer on this day as God adds air to the already existing water and light. Indeed, our God is a God who gives us life, makes it sustainable and helps it grow, and makes us beautiful.

However, perhaps the most significant characteristic of God we find on the second day is that He hates to be separated from His creation. Everything that God does throughout the rest of creation, indeed the rest of the meta-narrative of The Bible, is driven by this.

What an assurance it is for us, when we go through the same dislike of being separated from the people and the things that we love, that we can see we are actually experiencing a little bit of heavenly behaviour. This is a piece of the way God made us shining through.

It is also worth noting that God is more involved in this day. He does not command the waters to separate; He does not call an expanse into being. He does this Himself, with His own hands. The word for 'made' is 'asah', which equally means 'to fashion.' We can discern two things here. First, even though creating the expanse is marked with pain, it is a beautiful thing to behold, because it has been fashioned by God's own hand with care. And second, when it comes to the really big sacrifices, God turns up in person and carries them out Himself.

Honestly, how was Jesus ever a surprise? It's not like God kept this side of himself secret. He revealed it on page one!

As we read on through creation we will see many more separations, and most of them are full of obvious goodness - such as the separation of animals into their various kinds. Then, as the sixth day comes to its conclusion we will even begin see more clearly just how good this second day's moment of separation was.

However, it is built into the foundations of creation not to like the feeling of being separated from God. This second day was never going to feel like a good day, no matter how far God's good plan was advanced because of it in the long term. And it will never feel like a good day if we find ourselves separated from Him.

THE GOD OF PAGE ONE

7

THE
THIRD
DAY

And God said, "Let the waters under the heavens be gathered together ..."

Genesis 1 v 9

STUDY QUESTIONS (4)

Read Genesis 1 v 9-13.

Key question: How much difference does God's separation from creation make?

Why is it important that the earth has both land and water?

Who creates the vegetation? What do we learn about God from this?

Why does God create plants, "each according to its own kind"? Does this variety and complexity tell us anything about God, or about ourselves?

NOTES

AND SO we come to the third day, and immediately we see the acceleration in God's creative work. Up to this point each day has only sought to achieve one development in creation but from the third day onwards so much more happens.

It is like creation has gathered its own momentum and, like an avalanche, it inevitably gets faster and faster until it reaches its culmination. And it reverberates with God's love, as we sense the urgency He feels to reconnect with His creation.

The author of this account appears to recognise this acceleration by describing this day in terms of two distinct activities, both beginning with "And God said ..." and both incorporating all of the four stages of calling, affirming, separating and naming. This is a day with a double portion of purpose, of goodness, of variety and identity. This is a day when God's plan is reaffirmed twice as creation takes a giant leap forward.

So that we don't miss anything, let's zoom in and break this day down into the two stages that the Genesis author identifies:

And God said, "Let the water under the heavens be gathered together into one place, and let the dry land appear." And it was so. God called the dry land Earth, and the waters that were gathered together he called Seas. And God saw that it was good.

Genesis 1 v 9 - 10

When I read this account, yet again I get a strong sense of God the story-teller, who knows where He is leading us but only reveals one tantalising element at a time. And with each new element of creation a new aspect of His plan unfolds and a new side to His character is revealed.

Imagine you were the among first listeners to this account, picturing themselves alongside the angels as witnesses to the event itself. Imagine their confusion at the end of the second day: "What is He up to?" Then imagine their anticipation at this point when the earth really begins to take shape. They must have seen it by now: "Here are the building blocks for life!" Now the stage is set, the earth is recognisable as a habitat, and all that remains is for God to fill His creation with life.

As we have seen from the first two days, God is drawing chaos into order and setting the stage for life to abound in His created universe, with the establishment of water, light and air. This drawing out of order continues into the third day with the gathering together of the waters into seas.

Just as on the first and second days, we can see the relationship between God and His creation at work as He calls the waters to gather and the waters responds. And so immediately after God's separation from the heavens and the earth we see that it does not mean His isolation from them.

He is a God who may seem at a distance - may be out of sight - and yet He remains as intimately involved in His creation as ever, and His voice speaks just as clearly and just as powerfully to us, inviting us to join in His work and respond to Him in relationship.

Only this time the purpose of His calling out is not to separate God from the earth but to separate out the different realms of life. Water is always the source of life. This is a biological, a spiritual and a poetic truth. Without water life is impossible, but wherever there is water, life can emerge, life can be sustained and life can thrive.

Perhaps the number one priority in astronomy these days is to identify other worlds that have liquid water on them, because they know that where water is found, life is almost inevitable. Knowing this, perhaps God's intention for His creation should have been apparent to us from the very beginning.

The earth was destined to be a home for life from its first day as a swirling mass of water. By the third day that water had separated to reveal the sky and separated again to reveal the land, thereby establishing two new habitats for life that emerge from the life-giving water. And the word 'reveal' is important here. The sky and the land were already there, but they were overwhelmed by the chaos. Our God is a God who draws order from chaos to reveal the places He has already made where He will bring life.

In particular, this day is about establishing the habitat He has set aside for *our* life: the land. We will read how God began life on the land in just a moment, but that is very much in the second action of this day described by the author, as denoted by the second "And God said ..."

In this first action we are only told two things about the land. First, that it is "dry land." For us this is two words but in the Hebrew it is only one word - 'yabbashah' - but it is repeated, emphasising that this is dry and *firm* land. Our God is a God who gives us a firm foundation. The seas and the sky are shifting habitats but we are called to live life on solid ground. It is built into the foundations of creation that we live on the rock.

We are then told that God calls it "Earth." The word here is 'erets', which is a word that is used both to describe the whole Earth as a planet and it is also the word for "territory." In other words, it is defined by who lives there.

THE THIRD DAY

This gives us a wonderful insight into God's view of His creation. He calls it the Earth from verse one but it doesn't actually become the Earth until the land is revealed. Our God is a God who acts on vision and who confers identity on the work of His hands before it has fully assumed that identity.

How encouraging is this for us as we receive our identity as children of God even though we can see how little we seem to reflect that identity? God still looks on us and calls us His redeemed children because He can see what we will become, and where we will end up.

We can also see that God's plan was always for the Earth to be a dwelling place. Even in the darkness and the void God looked on the waters and saw a place where we could live. And so He named it based on what He could see it would become, but it was only as it became a habitable territory that it truly became what He had envisioned. With that in mind, let's focus in on the second stage of the third day:

And God said, "Let the earth sprout vegetation, plants yielding seed, and fruit trees bearing fruit in which is their seed, each according to its kind, on the earth." And it was so. The earth brought forth vegetation, plants yielding seed according to their own kinds, and trees bearing fruit in which is their seed, each according to its kind. And God saw that it was good. And there was evening and there was morning, the third day.
Genesis 1 v 11-13

117

At last life explodes onto the scene! And it really is an explosion. At the start of this day the Earth is still a desolate and lonely place, a swirling ball of chaotic water. By the end it is blue and green, fruitful and vivacious, with a power to recreate all of its own. As the evening draws in we have an Earth described that we would recognise.

As we listen to God's words we find that again He is inviting His creation to take part in His work. He does not create the plants, but invites the land to produce them: "Let the earth sprout vegetation." But we also see here that even this first form of life is given some of the power and purpose of God, as He issues the plants and fruit with the ability and charge to continue the growth of creation and the expansion of life. This is the first time we clearly see that God's nature is inherited by that which He creates.

And, of course, to the listener, that sense of purpose goes further than reproduction. There is first and foremost the purpose simply to be alive, to share in the world God has made; then, there is the purpose to sustain life, especially life beyond one's own; then, finally, there is the purpose to create life - a purpose that not only is at the heart of everything God does, but is also given by God to all life He creates.

What strikes me here as well is God's humility, revealed in His willingness to step aside as The Creator as He invites the life He has created to assume His responsibility and continue His creative work. This is something we see more and more from this point on, not only for the rest of this creative week[27], but throughout Scripture, as God refuses to impose Himself outside of invitation and relationship.

So God is a God who gives purpose and character according to Himself, and who is humble and releasing. He is also a God of extraordinary variety, complexity and precision. As God called the vegetation to life, He separated it into its various kinds. Here the listener's own knowledge takes over and further description is unnecessary. We are invited to consider the countless species, sub-species and varieties of plant-life on the Earth, how it all fits perfectly into its surroundings and contributes to the health of its environment, including the life of other plant-life.

This is an aspect of creation that only becomes more impressive the more we discover about the world. Never mind whether their creation happened in the glimpse of a moment or over a great length of time, every tiny piece in the massive jigsaw of organic life is called into being with both the character and purpose of God conferred upon it. There is nothing too small, nothing too insignificant, for God's considered attention.

Everything God makes has meaning and is important, and everything He makes is beautiful. And we have already seen that everything God makes is the way it is because of the way He is, so we

---

[27] We will explore this again on the fifth day and the arrival of more sophisticated animal life.

know that He is beautiful and He is complex and life-giving and life-sustaining and, most powerfully, He is alive.

8

THE FOURTH DAY

And God said, "Let there be lights in the expanse of the heavens ..."

Genesis 1 v 14

STUDY QUESTIONS (5)

Read Genesis 1 v 14-19.

How amazing must God have seemed at this moment to the original hearers of this story? Do we still feel that amazement?

Key question: what are the stars for?

What does this tell us about what God is like and how he sees us?

NOTES

AS THE drive towards order from chaos continues apace, with the waters having separated and gathered and the plants separating into their wondrous variety, the fourth day brings order to the light, which is given both constraint and function:

And God said, "Let there be lights in the expanse of the heavens to separate the day from the night. And let them be for signs and for seasons, and for days and years, and let them be lights in the expanse of the heavens to give light upon earth." And it was so. And God made the two great lights - the greater light to rule the day and the lesser light to rule the night - and the stars. And God set them in the expanse of the heavens to give light on the earth, to rule over the day and over the night, and to separate the light from the darkness. And God saw that it was good. And there was evening and there was morning, the fourth day.

Genesis 1 v 14-19

125

Until this point, light has been a constant presence, extending everywhere since God called it into being on the first day. However, in the vast emptiness of the universe there was no physical body except for the Earth, so that in almost the whole of creation nothing could be seen since light had so little to reveal after the separation of the waters and the establishment of the empty expanse on the second day.

Of course, the Earth had substance so it was fully lit and so God's work on the third day - the emergence of land and the explosion of life - happened whilst bathed in God's first expression of goodness and was a wonder to be witnessed. However, it was surrounded by an expanse of empty darkness.

On the fourth day God fills the expanse with stars - again calling them into being as creation responds to His voice - so that the whole of His creation might once again be seen. It is a dramatic image, and would have been all the more vivid to the first listeners who could look up and see a sky awash with stars and galaxies, uninhibited by light pollution, and could imagine the drama of them bursting into existence from the pitch darkness.

As they pictured this in their minds how could they not be gripped with wonder at their God, who had given them such a vast blanket of beauty and complexity? How could they not know how powerful, massive and awesome, and yet intricate and intimate God is? How could they not feel honoured above all creation to be at the centre of God's attention as He did this?

And they could be in no doubt that they were in the centre of God's attention, even before humanity had been created, and even if they were not, in fact, at the centre of the universe as was also commonly believed. They could be in no doubt because of the explicit purposes God gave to the stars: to separate day from night, to signify the seasons and to light the Earth.

All three of these purposes are expressly for the benefit of God's people on Earth. Yet again, we find God's plan at the forefront of our attention, as we see Him putting in place all the building blocks for sustainable life before humanity is introduced.

And so what do we learn from this critical step in God's plan? Well, here we begin to get a sense for the first time of how important we are within creation. This is before we are told that we are to rule over the animals and the plants, before we have even been conceived in this account, but we are told that the stars and galaxies are there to mark the seasons, to guide us at night, to help us find our place in the world. They are there to serve us in practical ways.

I have a fond memory of leading a youth bible study a few years ago and looking at this paragraph. I asked them what the universe, in all its vastness and majesty, was for. I will never forget the tone of the nervous voice that chanced an answer: "Is it to help us tell the time?" He felt foolish but at its simplest edge he was absolutely right. Here we have the most extraordinary, massive, awesome, spellbinding pocket watch!

The universe is given as a blessing to us for guidance, for timing, for rhythm of life. As we stand in time at the moment, this is one of those realisations that keep on giving! It would be easy to think that current scientific understanding only seems to belittle the earth, pushing it to the edge of an insignificant galaxy among billions of others, but really what this seems to do is show all the more how unique and extraordinary the earth is: the only place we have so far found life; more significantly, the only place with the urge to discover its purpose.

The bigger and more complex we discover the universe to be, the more significant it reveals us to be. God did all that for us! How much do we matter to him?!

Not only does this show us just how important we are in creation - which also tells us so much about how God is a God who will go to any lengths to bless and equip those whom He loves - but it also introduces us to our God who guides us. Think of the way humanity has instinctively looked to the stars for guidance throughout history. Without them we could not navigate the earth, we could not know our place in the universe, we would have no measure for time, and - surely most significantly - the wise men would never have realised that Jesus was to be born!

Of course, when God has been taken out of the equation the stars have been used for unhelpful and even destructive purposes too, expressed through astrology and the like[28], but still this concerns guidance. It is like the Chinese Whispers I suggested earlier - the essence remains, but without God the true joy of it is warped and lost.

Whether for good or evil, humanity has always naturally looked up to the stars for guidance, and the fourth day goes a long way to explaining why. It is part of purpose of creation to guide, because it reflects God's nature as a guide. Indeed, not only is God's presence as our guide reflected in the stars, His presence as our king is reflected in the sun and moon, as they are made to rule over the day and night and to separate light from darkness, again reinforcing God's ever-presence, His kingdom authority and His pursuit of the light in our lives.

It is significant that His kingly presence is another of the very few things He established with his own hands. The word 'asah' is used again here, as he fashions the sun and moon personally, placing His own kingship in the heavens - something creation could never do, as God remains unique in all creation because of His majesty.

---

[28] A friend once told me his zodiac sign was year of the horse. I don't he was missing anything significant.

The fourth day also shows us that God is a God who works in seasons, and that there is a healthy rhythm to His life. We see this reinforced often later in Scripture, such as the language of Ecclesiastes ('a time to ...') or Jesus' parable of the vine (John 15), not to mention the seventh day of creation, which we shall examine in chapter eleven. God has built the universe in such a way that his rhythm is conveyed to us and we fall in line with it.

And we learn so much about God from the seasons: He takes us through times of life and death, growth and pruning, hot and cold, light and dark, and so on and so on. This really is only saying what Jesus also said in John 15. His talking of being pruned back to the vine relies so much on our basic understanding of how creation works, as established on this fourth day.

It prompts the question: what is our rhythm of life like? It must be a critical question for us, because so much of this passage is about establishing God's love and majesty, His plan and his desire to have a relationship with creation, with us at the head of it, and to do this we must walk in step with him - in the same rhythm. And so the passage lays out a weekly rhythm, a seasonal rhythm, a creative rhythm, which if we live by we will find opens up our relationship with Him.

9

THE
FIFTH
DAY

*And God said, "Let the waters swarm with
swarms of living creatures, and let birds
fly above the earth ..."*

Genesis 1 v 20

STUDY QUESTIONS (6)

Read Genesis 1 v 20-23.

What impression do we get about God from how he creates life?

Key question: Is it significant that God blesses and commissions life on the fifth day, when he doesn't do the same on the third day?

How does God want life to influence the earth?

Why?

NOTES

IF THE third day is when life exploded onto the Earth, then the fifth day is when life completely redefined it. From here on the story of creation no longer concerns itself with the physical entity of the Earth and its place in the universe, or its relationship with the heavens; it now zooms in to see the Earth only through the lens of what inhabits it:

And God said, "Let the waters swarm with swarms of living creatures, and let birds fly above the earth across the expanse of the heavens." So God created the great sea creatures and every living creature that moves, with which the waters swarm, according to their kinds, and every winged bird according to its kind. And God saw that it was good. And God blessed them, saying, "Be fruitful and multiply and fill the waters in the seas, and let birds multiply on the earth." And there was morning and there was evening, the fifth day.

Genesis 1 v 20-23

135

We have already seen, before the first day and on the third day, how God had already named the Earth 'erets' - identifying it as a habitat and as a territory, and it is now that we see the Earth stepping into the vision God has had for it from its inception. It has always been the Earth because God called it so, and from the third day it has begun to look like the Earth, but only now does it begin to properly reflect its calling, as it begins to perform its purpose: to be the home for conscious sophisticated life.

As it does so, the first thing that strikes us is the abundance of its population. The ESV describes it in terms of swarming. The NIV describes it as teeming. The Hebrew word is 'sharrats', which precisely does mean to swarm and to teem ... and also to multiply.

We cannot escape the power involved in creating this massive scale of life, nor the sense of movement. The energy of it all, and the noise it conjures in the mind, is astonishing compared to the comparative quiet of creation up to this point. It's as if God began with, "Let there be light," moved on to, "Let there be beauty" and now crescendos with, "Let there be action!"

This is life that is uncontainable, irrepressible and unstoppable, exactly as God is. It has its own momentum and is gifted with the power to increase and spread across the whole world for all of time. As life fills the world God has prepared for it, there is also the sense is that the world itself also receives the blessing as the waters also swarm and teem and multiply. Creation is blessed as it steps into the purpose for which it was created.

In the midst of this we again find a humble God who is willing to stand back from taking the credit for every creation, as He releases first the plants and now the more sophisticated fish and birds to take part in the work that comes from His nature: that of creating life.

God is the source of all life, and so He has every right to be the one who gets to draw intimately close to the newborn and take joy in them, just as He did over the whole of creation. And yet He steps aside and gives that privilege to others. God is responsible for the life in my two daughters and yet He allows me to watch over them, to linger in their presence and raise them. He trusts me to invite Him in, but He does not impose Himself. This is a humility that becomes a hallmark of God's character in the years to come, and it is established here on page one.

Not only do we see the humility of God, we also see His generosity, through His desire to share the glorious fruit of His creativity. And it's not like He chose only a few to share it with - He so loves to share what is His that He fills the Earth with life to receive it.

God is a God who blesses in abundance, who seeks to fill every space with his goodness. He doesn't create a few, He creates swarms; and He doesn't ask them to be content, He commissions them to fill and to multiply ... to always reach beyond their borders and spread their life and influence across the whole world.

Again, as we saw on the fourth day, the intricacy and precision of all of this is breathtaking. This is the unspoken implication that no-one would have missed. They hear about the creatures of the sea and the winged birds - all "according to their kind" and surely they could not help but think of the variety that this encompasses, and the way in which each creature affects its environment and the other creatures around it.

Yet again, this is a revelation that only sharpens the more we discover about the world and the universe. The balance of life is perfect, because God is a God of perfection and precision. His plan is perfect and precise, down to the smallest detail, and He has created a world and life that works in perfect harmony, that sits in the perfect spot in the solar system to be protected and to be ideal for life to thrive.

God has placed everything exactly in the right place in the universe, and so how much more can we trust that He has placed us in exactly the right place in our lives as well?

We also find the relationship between God and His creation deepening here, reflected in the extended purpose given to the living creatures - to fill the earth. Up to this point the relationship has been relatively one-sided: God is the creator and the created things respond to Him. With the arrival of the first animals, however, this shifts as God blesses and commissions life with the power and responsibility to continue His work.

Now the relationship is more two-way, with God responding to life with blessing as life responds to Him.

This is a critical development in His plan, which is now getting very close to being fully unfolded, and it is significant that this deepened relationship is reflected in the nature of that which He creates. On the third day, plant life is also given the ability to reproduce, but it is not given the choice of whether to reproduce. Its seeds are a part of what it is, and they will fall with the seasons regardless.

With the creatures of the sea and the birds, as with the animals that follow on the sixth day, there is a greater degree of choice. It is now physically possible for these creatures not to reproduce, but God entrusts them with this freedom.

This is the first time we really see how God wants a relationship with Him to work - that He says how it should be, he demonstrates its value (in this instance through the fruitfulness of the plants), then He empowers that which He creates to reflect His behaviour, but without ever imposing Himself, so that a relationship with God is founded on walking with Him by choice, exercising free will and sharing in His liberty.

God is a God who empowers, who entrusts, who models (or, as Jesus might describe it, who disciples), and who gives freedom.

One final thought before we move on: why does it say, "God saw that it was good" and not, "God saw that they were good?" What is the "it?" This has been a background niggle in the previous days, but is most obvious on this fifth day, because there is no way of saying that God only creates one thing here - the extraordinary variety across two separately described environments of the sea and the sky surely can only be seen in the plural.

I'm always pretty delighted when I find a question like this that I can't quite put my finger on, because it's so good to recognise where I've still got a long way to dig. There is yet more treasure to find! This is a question I've not yet reached the bottom of, but so far I can think of three possibilities, all of which tell us something about God.

First, it might be creation as a whole. After every new stage of creation God stands back, looks at creation and sees that it is good. It continues to respond in relationship and to reflect His character and it grows ever more beautiful as it grows closer to walking in its purpose. This reveals the God of love, who continually looks back at His beloved creation and takes new joy in the goodness of it whenever He does so.

Second, perhaps it is God's plan coming into being. At the end of each day He looks at what He has achieved and He sees that it is still perfectly on course for His grand plan to share eternity with humanity, surrounded by life and all the beauty He can muster, and His plan is good. This reveals the God of eternity, who looks across time and sees what is to come and delights in the prospect of sharing all He has with us forever.

Lastly, perhaps it is God's word. Each day He calls creation into being and as creation responds to His voice and His heart's desire fills the world, He can see the strength of relationship and the fruit of creation and He knows His word is good. This reveals the God of power, whose voice calls the heavens and the earth into being, in all its vastness and all its precision, speaking out all the strength of His kingdom.

Grammatically, I tend towards the last but I am enthusiastic to believe all of them, since they reveal the three fundamental aspects of God's nature (love, eternity and power) which usher us into a relationship with Him and which were established in the beginning, before the first day.

THE GOD OF PAGE ONE

10

THE SIXTH DAY

And God said, "Let the earth bring forth living creatures ..."

Genesis 1 v 24

STUDY QUESTIONS (7)

Read Genesis 1 v 24-31.

Why are the animals identified in the three broad categories of livestock, creeping things and beasts of the earth?

What is so different about these animals that they are created separately from the fish and birds?

What does this all tell us about who God is?

Key question: How does God's identity shift when humanity joins the party?

Is the timing of man's creation, at the end of the sixth day, significant?

NOTES

WHEN WE read the sixth day it is all too easy for our eye to be drawn to the creation of humanity, because here the onus seems to shift away from telling us about God to telling us about, well, us. We can also feel the first few verses are easy to skip, since they seem only to repeat, more or less, what has already been said on the fifth day.

However, the sixth day is just as rich in new revelation about who God is as the rest of the creation week. In fact, it can be broken down into three distinct sections, which together make up an action-packed day. More happens on this day than on any other. First, there is the creation of the land-living creatures, next the creation of man and finally the blessing of both.

In this chapter we will take each in turn, but so that our eye is not drawn prematurely, and because I want us to look at how man is established separately, we are going to limit our view of verses 26-29 to one principal revelation and will return to this segment in chapter ten.

So, let us begin by paying attention to how the land-dwelling creatures are made:

> *And God said, "Let the earth bring forth living creatures according to their kinds - livestock and creeping things and beasts of the earth, according to their kinds." And it was so. And God made the beasts of the earth according to their kinds and the livestock according to their kinds, and everything that creeps on the ground according to its kind. And God saw that it was good . . .*

Genesis 1 v 24-25

As we read this we instantly see the relationship between God and His creation reinforced as he calls the earth to bring forth the living creatures and the earth responds. Indeed, we see so much of what we have already learned about God reinforced: the power of His voice, His humble inclusion of creation in His work, the diversity of His vision, His wisdom and willingness to separate creatures according to their kinds, the inherent goodness of His labour, all resulting in a creation that reflects its creator.

But we see new things too. For a start, although God does invite the earth to "bring forth" the living creatures (the word used is *yatsa* - literally "to come out") in verse 24, in verse 25 it goes on to say that God "made the beasts of the earth according to their kinds." The word for "made" here is *asah* (to fashion), which as you will remember is the same word used to describe God creating the expanse with his own hands on the second day.

So, what do we make of this? Does the earth or God take the initiative in creating the land animals? Well, of course, it is God's word that takes the initiative, speaking out his will and design, but verse 24 seems to make it clear that the earth has an integral part to play in the physical act of creation, just as it has in the creation of plant-life.

However, as the earth's remit for joining in with God is extended, what it cannot do is take responsibility for the diversity of these conscious beings, since this also speaks to the purpose for each creature in a way that it did not for the plants (although they too are created with variety), and the focus of verse 25 seems to be on God's direct role in the variety of life. It is the "according to their kinds" distinction that God introduces with his own hands.

So, what we find here is a partnership between God and his creation, another level of detail exposed concerning God's priority for, love of and use of relationship with his creation. The earth brings forth life, and God gives it purpose, found in the unique identities of each species.

To dig into this further we might consider more closely the creatures that are created, particularly how they are categorised: livestock, creeping things and beasts of the earth. It would not be difficult for any of us to break the animal kingdom down into more specific classes, so we must assume that there is something particularly significant about these types of creatures to the original tellers and receivers of this story.

So what is it about livestock, creeping things and beasts of the earth? Well for one thing, they each had a big impact on people's lives, but in very different ways.

Imagine you were among the first people hearing this account, however many thousands of years ago. What would you think about when you heard livestock named? These were animals that were subservient to man, and which man relied on for survival. How about creeping things? In the hot climates of Africa and the Near East, these would have been a constant pest and, depending on the season, a regular threat to crops and health. And then there are the beasts of the earth, the predators, which were a constant danger in the harsh environment they lived in.

These creatures are all defined by their relationship to man. In other words, they draw attention to the aspects of man's life that they affect, and so draw attention to how God responds to those aspects, having put these creatures in man's way, yet given man dominion over them. Livestock represents livelihood and blessing, creeping things represent trials and seasons, and beasts of the earth represent dangers and risk. These would have made up the most dominant considerations in a family's life, and here we have God in authority over all of them - He is the king of every aspect of our lives.

Furthermore, we have a God who knows everything that we face, who provides for us (including his protection) but does not withhold us from trials and dangers. Why not? Because how else can we receive the fullness of His promise to us in creation? God holds nothing back, and He invites us to share in and rule over everything He has made. There may be dangers and trials, but they are set in a world that is good, and which has blessing and provision gifted by God.

We see from page one that God has created a system in which we are safe and fruitful so long as we receive His blessing and remain in His company. This is a critical foundation of the Kingdom of God that is laid here: that we get to share in all of God's creation - even the bits that could be dangerous for us - so long as we walk with Him, knowing God as both provider and protector - Jehovah Jireh and Jehovah Nissi.

Already a world has been created where self-reliance is a dangerous thing and God-reliance is where true freedom lies. Only with God is everything He made a wonder we can all share.

Think ahead to Noah. What we see is a man who walks so closely with God that the "dangerous beasts" do not harm him and he is able to rule over them as God intended. This was always the plan, and this is the environment that God has created. It is a world where, if we walk away from God we are in peril, but if we walk with Him we are in beauty.

So, we read how this environment is completed on the sixth day and we find a God who offers complete freedom and access to Him and all His fruit. We find a God who knows our needs, our frustrations and our dangers, and wants to walk with us through all of them as creator and companion, provider and protector.

And then we should ask why it is that God calls forth the creatures of the land last. A scientific observation might be that it mimics the approximate order of the evolution of life as it is currently understood. Perhaps, although hardly precisely. Or perhaps this is over-thinking it a little, and that really what is being told to us here is that as God builds towards the completion of His plan, which by now is surely an inescapable process in the listener's mind, that He is getting ever closer to the summit of His work.

Plant life is beautiful, complex, fascinating and irrepressible, but ultimately it is established on day three to serve something that is yet to come and we must wait to find out what.

The fish and the birds are a giant leap forward in the complexity of life, and they contribute to the sustenance of the environment in extraordinary ways as they cultivate the plants and maintain the waters.

But it is with the land animals that we see life being given a purpose to serve man - including livestock being named as such (i.e. as a creature destined to be farmed) before man has even arrived - and all being described in terms of how they relate to man. As such, these creatures are not given the same instruction as the birds and the sea creatures to swarm and fill their environment. If they did, there would be no room for one last set of residents, and there really must be room for them.

For six days God has been building towards something, and now we get a clear glimpse of what it is: these are creatures that are defined by how they impact us, and it is this observation that ushers us onto the scene, as we see a cosmos and a world that has now been completed and is ready to receive the last inhabitant that everything so far has been created to bless and serve.

So let us move on to that ultimate moment in creation's journey: humanity finally joining the party:

Then God said, "Let us make man in our image, after our likeness. And let them have dominion over the fish of the sea and over the birds of the heavens and over the livestock and over all the earth and over every creeping thing that creeps on the earth." So God created man in his own image, in the image of God he created him; male and female he created them. And God blessed them. And God said to them, "Be fruitful and multiply and fill the earth and subdue it and have dominion over the fish of the sea and over the birds of the heavens and over every living thing that moves on the earth."
Genesis 1 v 26-28

153

All of creation has been leading to this point. As soon as humanity arrives on the scene creation shifts from object to subject, and is only described in relation to the new object of God's attention.

We will look at what this reveals about humanity separately but for the time being, just consider what it is that man first knows. He sees none of the formation of the heavens and the earth, hears none of the authoritative commands of Creator God. Instead, he sees a complete environment, ready for him to dwell in, and he sees the one who made him, and he hears the voice of blessing, as his creator looks on him in love for the first time.

This is the moment that God's revelation of Himself moves beyond His character and into His identity. So far His primary identity has been Creator, as He has called creation into being and the fabric of creation has responded.

The only parts of creation God has so far made by His own hands (remember that word 'asah' - to fashion) are the expanse on the second day, as He sacrificed His own presence so that we might rule over creation, the sun and moon on the fourth day, as His light is given jurisdiction in all times, and the beasts on this sixth day, though only in partnership with the land. Now that same word is used again as God fashions man with His own hands.

The earth plays no part in the creation of this life. The only connection is between God and man. There is a more personal touch from God in this action, because there is to be a more personal connection between Him and this new inhabitant of the world. This is the physical connection between a father and his child.

To the rest of creation, God is Creator; to us He is Father. And in this moment of intimacy we see a loving father talking to his child for the first time, with words of blessing and with words of inheritance, as He describes how man will do the same things in the world as God has been doing - and not just *some* of the same things, as the plants and animals are to do, but *all* of the same things: communing with God *and* creating life *and* subduing the earth. More on this in chapter ten.

And what does man look like? He looks like his father. Again, we will consider this more closely in chapter ten, because it is this characteristic above all other that reveals who God has made us to be and how our relationship with Him is intended to be expressed. However, we cannot escape the simple genetic observation: we look like Him. The Genesis author emphasised this point - not only are we made "in his image" but we are also made "after his likeness." Very simply, physically, spiritually, emotionally, behaviourally, we look like our dad.

And who is our dad? He is the Creator, the King, the all-powerful God, who will move heaven and earth, incredibly literally, to make sure we have the best home to grow up in and the best future to step into.

And what is our dad like? He is loving and powerful, authoritative and kind, holy and constant, gracious and humble, purposeful and perfect; He is to be feared and yet He invites us into the intimacy of His presence. And He is always there, and He always will be.

This is what our Father looks like, and certainly this is what his son Jesus looked like. Well, we are also his sons and daughters and so we are to look like this too. Genesis 1 is not only a revelation of our Father; it is a vision for our own lives. Is this the side of us the world sees?

Our creation at the end of the sixth day was so perfectly placed, not only because now our environment is perfect to welcome us, but most especially because it meant our first sight of God was as our father. The rest of creation must look on God and see its creator but God always intended us to see Him first as our Father and for our relationship with Him to be founded on that revelation. Sadly, events in Eden drew us away from this place of intimacy and even today it is so rare that the first way we see God is as our loving heavenly Father.

All that said, it must be acknowledged that many scholars would sway against me a little on this one. Their assertion would be that Genesis 1 reveals God the architect more than it does the king or the father, both of which are revealed more richly in Genesis 2 and 3, and even then God's fatherhood doesn't take root as a common theological concept until the New Testament.

Certainly, God's identity as king and father are much more obvious in the days of Eden, and the overt understanding of God as a father is notably quiet throughout much of the Old Testament[29], but I don't think that this necessarily detracts from their presence here, as we see God towering in majesty over creation, and blessing his children in the same way that the family of God continues to bless their offspring for the generations to come.[30]

It may also be reasonably argued, as I discussed in chapter one, that what was obscure in the days of its writing are given new clarity in the light of Jesus, who revealed God as Father in a way that had never been fully acknowledged before. But then, in John 8:41, the Pharisees themselves described God as their Father as they objected to Jesus' description of them as children of evil, which in itself demonstrates that the view of God as Father was familiar in Jesus' day; but he readjusted the focus, so that God might once again be viewed by man as a Father first, then as the King and Creator, just as was the case in Genesis 1.

---

[29] Quiet, but not absent. In Isaiah 63 v16 we read: "You O LORD, are our Father, our Redeemer from of old is your name;" consider also Psalm 139 v13-14 and Isaiah 44 v2, which describe God's creative involvement in the womb; or God's pleading to Israel, who he calls his "faithless daughter" in Jeremiah 31 v22; or how about Hosea 11 v1: "When Israel was a child I loved him, and out of Egypt I called my son" or Malachi 2 v10: "Have we not all one father? Has not one God created us?"

[30] For example, the blessing Isaac speaks over his son Jacob in Genesis 27:27-29 has, to my mind, a very similar feel, with similar priorities forming its heart.

And so, as we now look back, we can see more than was obvious at the time. God does not change, and so he is as much the Father in Genesis 1 as he is anywhere else, but it can be seen so much more sharply now that Jesus has cast light in that direction.

I should also note that I am not a lone voice on this side of the debate, and others have offered their own evidence to support a claim of fatherhood here. For example, Carly Crouch (lecturer in Hebrew Bible at the University of Nottingham), in her article *Genesis 1:26-7 as a Statement of Humanity's Divine Parentage*[31], proposes more evidence that this passage reveals a fatherly God.

In particular, she focuses on the use of the word 'tselem' (which we will examine more closely in the next chapter) and the word 'demuwth' which together shape the phrases "in our image" and "after our likeness." She notes how these words make it clear that God is describing the physical similarity I mentioned earlier - man looks like God, just as a child looks like their parent.

She goes on to describe how the exact same words are also used to describe Adam fathering his son Seth in Genesis 5 v3. In this case, the words are clearly used to describe the parental lineage, and there can surely be no doubt that Genesis 5 v1 is deliberately quoting Genesis 1 v26-7, which is a compelling argument to suggest that it is the same essence of

---

[31] Journal of Theological Studies, volume 61, Oxford Journals, 2010, p.1-15.

parent to child lineage being described, with the same passing on of identity, authority and character.

She also points to several other places in Scripture (some of which I also referenced in footnote 29) and other literary evidence from this point in history, when God was clearly identified as Father. This is not to diminish God's considerable identity as cosmological architect at all, but it seems to me that there is a good argument to see a father first, determining the framework for our relationship with him, followed by the architect and king and creator, which determine the framework of our responsibility with him over creation.

Finally, let us examine the blessing that God gives to the animals after man has been created:

And to every beast of the earth and to every bird of the heavens and to everything that creeps on the earth, everything that has the breath of life, I have given every green plant for food." And it was so. And God saw everything that he had made, and behold, it was very good. And there was evening and there was morning, the sixth day.

Genesis 1 v 30-31

Having first encountered God as our father, here we get the clearest vision of God as our provider. Before we got here, before even the animals, birds or fish got here, God had provided all that we needed to survive, to thrive and to have a sense of purpose, as we worked the land and cultivated the food we had been given. Again, here we see a God who knows our every need before we do and who has the solution if only we will listen to His voice as He blesses us and reveals His provision.

The key observation here is that His provision is in place before we need it, and so we discover a God who builds structure first and only then invites life to inhabit it.

I must confess at this point that this specific observation - structure before life - is one that was very recently highlighted to me by a colleague, who had in turn been challenged by a blog, which was in turn inspired by a book. I love how God gets the word around! As such it is still somewhat a thought in process for me, but since it is clearly both relevant and helpful, I shall briefly share where I am up to with it.

The book was *Multiplying Missional Leaders*[32] by Mike Breen, the blog was written by Ben Sternke[33], a church planter from Indiana, USA, and my colleague was Jo Pestell, director of operations at Westminster Theological Centre.

Between these three people, they have drawn attention to several subtler characteristics of God, which are revealed within the more dominant vision

---

[32] Mike Breen, *Multiplying Missional Leaders: From Half-hearted Volunteers to a Mobilised Kingdom Force*, 3DM, 2012

[33] The post is called "Which Comes First: Structure or Life?" and was written in March 2012 by Ben Sternke on his blog (www.bensternke.com)

of Him as Jehovah Jireh[34], our provider: that He prepares well, He does things perfectly, He has an immaculate sense of timing; He invites life - and therefore us - into completed places, and that His provision, His protection and His invitation to share everything that He has are rooted in creating the right environment.

This in turn highlights a significant implication from creation for how we in turn view our expressions of the Kingdom. The temptation can be to look for the life and then build structure around it; but the foundations of creation are laid by God having a vision for the life and building a complete structure for it to inhabit before its introduction. This, of course, is possible because God knows the right structure to build, which will bless and be blessed by the life it serves.

People tend not to be so knowledgeable. Anyone who has planted churches, started small groups, or done anything in any way pioneering in the church will know that most of the time it feels like thrashing around in the dark. In such times, the easier thing is to look for the life that already exists, but it needn't be that way.

If we are seeking vision, asking God for eyes to see Him and ears to hear Him, looking and listening for

[34] This identity given to God - one of seven 'redemptive names of God' - literally means 'The One who provides' and is first established by Abraham in Genesis 22 after God's provision of a ram as a sacrifice in place of his son Isaac.

answers from God's Word, His Spirit and His church, and if that vision is founded on who God is and who we are, as well as being driven by who we are extending His Kingdom to, and why (as opposed to "How do we do it, and when?"), then we are in a place of faith where we can expect life to fill - even to "swarm" - the structures we build. The trick is to ensure those structures are organic and fit for purpose.

However, here we are creeping into strategy and 'how' thinking instead of concentrating on the God who stands behind it, who displays this perfect order and provision. In any case, Mike's book and Ben Sternke's blog say it far better and I urge you to explore these essential questions more with them.

For now, let's conclude by looking back at God as He looks over His completed work. In this moment we find God in His most reflective mood, as He stands back and looks at everything He has done and takes delight in it.

He determines that every piece is in place, it all works, and it all serves those He made it all to share with: us. And with us in place, as His image before creation, He looks on it and sees that it is very good, we are very good, His plan, to rule over creation through us, is perfect and very good.

And because everything God has made is as it is because of whom God is, we can know with absolute certainty that God is very good.

11

INTRODUCING THE IMAGE

Then God said, "Let us make man in our image, after our likeness."

Genesis 1 v 26

STUDY QUESTIONS (8)

Read Genesis 1 v 26-28.

Key question: What does it mean to be the image of God?

How does God want a relationship to work between: a) God and creation; b) God and humanity?

What are the blessings/commissions given to the image of God, and how are we to express them?

What does this tell us about God?

NOTES

THERE IS still more to discover about God on the seventh day, but we must pause a moment here and revisit God's commission to man on the sixth day. Let's remind ourselves of what God said:

Then God said, "Let us make man in our image, after our likeness. And let them have dominion over the fish of the sea and over the birds of the heavens and over the livestock and over all the earth and over every creeping thing that creeps on the earth." So God created man in his own image, in the image of God he created him; male and female he created them. And God blessed them. And God said to them, "Be fruitful and multiply and fill the earth and subdue it and have dominion over the fish of the sea and over the birds of the heavens and over every living thing that moves on the earth."

Genesis 1 v 26-28

This is the moment when we finally understand the mystery of the "not good" second day, as it becomes

167

clear that for God's precise plan to work He needed to be separated from creation yet intimate with humanity, and so the physical expanse had to be created. And it is at this point that God can finally feel the full joy of His plan coming together, with Himself reconnected with creation, through the intimate relationship with man, and so it is no wonder He names it as very good.

There is a significant shift in the story at this point. As we have already examined, here we have the moment where God's identity shifts from Creator and King to Father, and everything that follows - from the blessings at the end of the sixth day that we have already read, to the revelations of the seventh day - must all be seen in the context of a father speaking over his son and modelling the life that the son must live. God's creation is complete and now His parenting and discipling begins.

The turning point is in God's affirmation of man's identity and purpose: to be the image of God. This is a concept that can be hard to get a hold on, and it is another example from creation where there is considerable disagreement. Is this a call to live as God would live, to reflect His character? Or is this a description of how we are innately created - so it is in our nature to be like God rather than an invitation - and only sin gets in the way of us seeing it? Or is it not so much about us as about God? Is this a revelation of what He physically looks like? Can it be all of these, or something else entirely?

INTRODUCING THE IMAGE

What do you think of when you hear the phrase 'image of God'? What does it mean to you to be made in the image of God? Why not take a few minutes to ponder this.

NOTES

The image of God means ...

Were you to discuss this passage in a bible study group, it is likely that you would now share a range of opinions, most of which would likely be pretty solid. The same is true of the theological community. Books have been written, sermons delivered, arguments forged, all of which bring some revelation to what is being described here. But to expect anyone to reveal it all is, I imagine, asking a little too much!

This is one of those times where God's words go so much further than we can fully comprehend, but the more we all dig in and add to the debate, the more revelation is exposed and the bigger our calling before God becomes. The meaning of life is probably just about the oldest, most disputed mystery there is. It is a unifying conundrum between faiths, cultures, believers and atheists alike, and here lies the answer. We are created to be the image of God.

As I say, so much has been written about this by wiser men than me, so I will limit my own comments to three observations which impact me most when I read this, which are, I would suggest, the three identifying and defining marks of what it means to be the image of God.

We have seen continually throughout the six days so far that creation is the way that it is because of who God is and what He is like. In particular, we saw how on the third, fifth and sixth days life is blessed to share in some of God's behaviour, as creation reflects its creator and the plants and animals are given the power to create life; and how animal life - that is, conscious life - is also given the physical ability to opt out, and thereby demonstrate a value of relationship by choosing to live in God's ways.

This too is a reflection of who God is. He is a God who freely chooses to create, to share and to bless; and who freely chooses to sacrifice Himself in order to elevate His most beloved children. All creation is as it is because of who God is, and man is no different.

So, as we read these verses, and we hear God describing who He has made us to be as He blesses and commissions us, we must be looking for how our calling is to reflect God's nature. This means that even though our focus here shifts from revealing who God is to revealing who we are, we are continuing to learn more about God's character.

These three verses reveal one of the most critical moments in all God's story. It is a moment when the meta-narrative is at the forefront of God's mind. He is not only revealing Himself, but also revealing us and how we are to have a relationship with Him; and as we read, we discover that the image of God is given three commissions, all of which are to behave as God behaves.

The first is to **commune with God**. Now straight off the bat you might take issue with me here. "Where does it say that, then?" would be a reasonable question. Well, I'm glad you asked! To answer this, it is important that we don't read this passage in isolation from the rest of Scripture (always a pretty

171

sound principle!) and we must also dig a little deeper than English translations of the Bible tend to allow. Specifically, we must look closer at the word 'image'.[35] The word in Hebrew is 'tselem', and it is a word used several times throughout the Old Testament. Let me give you a few examples:

> *Then all the people of the land went to the house of Baal and tore it down; his altars and his images* (tselem) *they broke in pieces.*

2 Kings 11 v 18

> *His beautiful ornament they used for pride, and they made their abominable images* (tselem) *and their detestable things of it.*

Ezekiel 7 v 20

---

[35] It is also imperative that I give due credit here to Crispin Fletcher-Louis, who has had a significant impact on how I read this. As principal and lecturer at Westminster Theological Centre, Crispin has taught about the image of God considerably more extensively than I am about to, specifically in regard to the application of the Hebrew word 'tselem'. That's not to say that he will agree with all of my conclusions, but so much of my perspective on this has been honed by Crispin that I cannot claim it as my own. As I write this he is in the process of writing two books on this subject, both of which will be must reads, but in the meantime the best current source for further study on this is to be found in his article 'God's Image, His Cosmic Temple and the High Priest: Towards an Historical and Theological Account of the Incarnation', published in *Heaven on Earth: The Temple in Biblical Theology* (edited by S. Gathercole and T. D. Alexander, published by Paternoster, 2004, pp.81-100).

INTRODUCING THE IMAGE

You shall take up Sikkuth your king, and Kiyyun your star-god - your images (tselem) that you made for yourselves.

Amos 5 v 26

In each of these cases we find the word 'tselem' is translated as 'image' just as it is in Genesis 1. However, I imagine you can already see that the word 'tselem' has quite a different meaning in these passages; but just to reinforce this, and to help us see even more clearly what we are talking about here, let's read each of those examples again, as translated in the New International Version (NIV):

All the people of the land went to the temple of Baal and tore it down. They smashed the altars and idols (tselem) to pieces.

2 Kings 11 v 18 (NIV)

They were proud of their beautiful jewellery and used it to make their detestable idols (tselem) and vile images.

Ezekiel 7 v 20 (NIV)

You have lifted up the shrine of your king, the pedestal of your idols (tselem), the star of your god - which you made for yourselves.

Amos 5 v 26 (NIV)

173

In fact, most English translations prefer to translate 'tselem' as 'idol' rather than 'image' in these instances. Furthermore, the description of the image of God in Genesis 1 seems to be one of only two occasions [36] in which 'tselem' is not used in the context of either idol worship or the hollowness of Godless people.[37] On the face of it, this seems to radically change the tone of God's words, from encouraging his children to be like Him, to suggesting they are somehow connected to idolatry. So, how do we resolve this problem?

First, we must forget all the negative connotations we carry of what an idol represents. Just as we should never read Scripture in isolation from the rest of Scripture, we should also never read it in isolation from the world in which it was birthed.

This is not to suggest that the words do not have power on their own merit (of course they do), but as we dig deeper it is very helpful to know about any cultural implications that were obvious at the time, needing no explanation, so that they remained unspoken assumptions in Scripture, but which have since been lost over time so that we no longer assume them.

One such example of this is how idols were understood. As we read the Bible today we get the

---

[36] Along with Genesis 9:6, which uses the word in the same context as in Genesis 1

[37] For example, Psalm 39 v6, where man is described as a "mere phantom (tselem)."

gist - idol worship is bad, because it is putting something hollow in place of God, thereby diminishing Him and enabling man to be the controlling influence between him and his deity. But this specifically concerns false idols and false gods. It's just that we only get one description of a genuine idol, and because we translate it as 'image' we tend not to see it.

So, what was an idol? The two beliefs we tend to hold these days are either that idols were simply representations of a god, so that people had something physical to focus on when they worshipped and prayed, or that people believed they were actually the god themselves, suggesting they were deluded, either by religious fervour or megalomania (since it would mean that God was fashioned by them, not the other way around).

In fact, neither of these is completely true, but both contain a kernel of truth.

The contemporary belief was that an idol was made by man, whether out of gold or bronze or wood or stone or whatever, and once it was finished the god it represented would actually, physically come and inhabit the statue.

So, to all intents and purposes, the idol became the god, whereby it could connect with its people. Therefore, naturally, the people would worship it, pray to it, seek its blessing and make sacrifice to it, as they looked beyond the physical material to the divinity within.

So, how does this passage, or indeed how do any of the tselem passages I have highlighted, look now if we plug this piece of information in?

We are not looking at God raising any comparisons with false idols. In fact, we discover one of the most amazing revelations about both God and ourselves: God's plan for creation was always that He lives in us and rules through us, as we do the things He does and are transformed to look like He does.

In our New Covenant days this is not particularly controversial theology. We are very familiar with the idea of God dwelling in us, in the form of the Holy Spirit, transforming us to His likeness and character, releasing His power through us and extending the borders of His kingdom before us.

What *is* amazing is that this was always Plan A. The New Covenant didn't change the terms of our relationship, it restored them back to how they were intended to be in the beginning, before the Eden debacle.

What is also amazing is how quickly God's people seem to have lost sight of this, so that by the time of Jesus' incarnation it appears to have been misunderstood by, or perhaps misrepresented to, the everyday Jewish believer, so that Jesus' teaching and understanding of how a relationship with God should be were shocking as much as restorative.

It also explains why God is so offended by false idols, not only because He is a jealous God and He knows the harm it causes us when we diminish Him, but also because we are diminishing and dishonouring ourselves. And both result in God's presence, God's power and God's kingdom being stifled.

Man is made in the image of God - as the idol of God - not merely His representative, but His face in the world, and his dwelling place. God will exercise His kingly authority over creation through man and woman by living in them, making them a holy people, set apart to carry and release His presence and power, and by establishing an intimate relationship with them, in which God and humanity talk and walk together in communion.

Being the image of God means being physically and actually connected to God, being the house for an uncontainable God who sacrificially gave up his earthly throne so we could sit in it and then humbly contained Himself within us so that we might rule out of righteousness. That connection is established with words of blessing, the first of many that we are to exchange with Him as we commune with Him.

Being the image of God also means doing the things He does, because we are not only to be His representative but also His reflexion and His regent, and so we commune with God because God communes with Himself.

God is a God of community. We have already observed, on the first day, that from the beginning God's name makes it clear that He is a plural. This is reinforced in His referring to Himself as "us" repeatedly throughout the chapter, especially when we note that this is not God speaking about Himself but speaking among Himself.

God is Himself a community and He knows that goodness is found when His power is expressed right across the community. It is just that before we come along, His community is three. But after humanity was formed, revealing God as Father, God's community grew and He commissioned them to be His image, to look like Him in and before the world, so that when the world saw man, it looked beyond the material to the Spirit within and saw God – not just in character but in physical form - doing as He does, beginning with a communion of blessing.

So that is the first mark of the image of God: communion. The remaining two are more obvious, because they come directly from God's spoken commission, and again both reflect what we have seen God doing throughout the first six days. God has created people to share in His glory and creation and so He wants to share everything He has with us - including His power and His responsibilities - and the second and third marks of the image of God relate to both of these.

The second part of humanity's commission to be the image of God is to **create life**:

"Be fruitful and multiply and fill the earth ..."

178

INTRODUCING THE IMAGE

This is a commission we share with all conscious living things, but as we have already established, humanity is given the most freedom to resist this calling. Animals have the physical ability to resist, but their instinct is so strong, and their identity is so connected to this responsibility that in reality it pretty much always overpowers their free will. Not so for humanity. Our distinction from the rest of creation lies in the extent of our free will, in our ability to have a fully chosen two-way relationship with the One whom we commune with.

But this is more than a revelation of free will. God describes creating life in three stages, each of them a blessing. Let's take them in turn. First, God wants us to be fruitful. Fruit is such a common biblical metaphor, but we mustn't let familiarity hold us back from fully appreciating and enjoying what God is saying to us.

We could leave it as "God wants us to be successful." That in itself is quite an observation, and one that many people struggle to accept. But God goes even further. He wants us to be fruitful. Fruit is the way that plants and trees create life by passing on the best of themselves.

God's purpose for our lives is to reproduce the most beautiful and nourishing parts of ourselves. This is what gives life to those around us as our hearts reproduce; this is what gives identity to our children as our bodies reproduce. And all this is possible because we have already had the most beautiful and nourishing presence and power of God planted in us, because our fruit is every part of our life that has been transformed by God, restored to its original beauty.

Then there is the blessing to multiply. God wants our fruit to spread, and He wants it to be in abundance. If it were simply a case of passing it on to our children then it would look more like addition, but God speaks of multiplication. He wants our "success" - our fruit, our beauty - to influence everyone around us, not only our children, and to be replicated in them. He wants our life - and therefore His presence within us - to spread across the earth and into the lives of those around us, so that what is in us is multiplied across creation and everyone might be blessed to live in relationship with God, in His freedom, and become fruitful themselves.

Finally, there is the blessing to "fill the earth." He wants us to be everywhere so that He can be everywhere. This is to be our response to a God who has such an adventurous spirit and such a desire to bless and rule over the whole earth that He wants us to extend our influence and our presence to fill the earth so that through us He might extend His influence, power and presence across creation.

This chimes so harmoniously with God's assurance many years later through Jeremiah: "I know the plans I have for you, declares the Lord, plans for welfare and not for evil, to give you a future and a hope"[38] and also through the words of Paul, written

---

[38] Jeremiah 29 v11

centuries later still, describing our God who "is able to do far more abundantly than all that we ask or think, according to the power at work within us."[39]

But then of course, as we have already discovered in Genesis 1 v1, God does not change, so naturally He continues to look on His children with the same desire for them to be fruitful, the same intention of enabling them to be so, and the same promise to multiply His blessing to fill the earth.

Let's move on to the third and final calling of humanity's commission to be the image of God: to **subdue the earth**. God says to us:

> "... Fill the earth and subdue it and have dominion over the fish of the sea and over the birds of the heavens and over every living thing that moves on the earth."

We are to subdue the earth as God subdues the earth, lovingly. We tend to hear the word subdue and see it as an oppressive action instead of a loving one but God subdues the earth by creating it according to His order and He wants to rule it according to His love. We are given that charge, to rule over all living things, to subdue the earth, on His behalf.

Just as with the first two commissions, this means more than reflecting Him, more even than representing Him. We are to rule like Him, behave

---

[39] Ephesians 3 v20

like Him, display His form and His character, and administer His power and His love, so that when He inhabits us He is relating to His creation just as He was able to when He hovered over the waters of the deep, before the first day.

This way, God's perfect plan is made real, as He maintains His rightful place as a loving King and Creator over creation, and a loving King and Father over us.

In response, we can expect the world to see beyond us to God within us and to serve and honour its king. The implications of this are massive, and they explain so many of the miracles throughout God's Word to come. Put most simply, the earth being subdued means that it will do as it is told.

When Jesus spoke about moving mountains[40], I don't believe he was only speaking metaphorically, although it certainly does have a powerful metaphorical application. I believe that he knew that he was the image of God - the second Adam as Paul identifies him[41] - and that of course the world would see God within him, would honour its king, and would do as it was told.

As the perfect image of God, he communed with his Father, following His ways and administering His will, multiplying life in the hearts of so many people and subduing the earth lovingly. Of course the mountains would move.

---

[40] Matthew 17 v20
[41] 1 Corinthians 15 v47

Similarly for the water Jesus walked on. He needed to get from one side of the lake to the other, why would he walk around, especially when his best friends were on the water? Of course the water would hold him. Or with healings: of course tissue would right itself, of course optic nerves would reconnect, of course bones would realign.

Ever since those remarkable days, the church has been home to many such testimonies, as communities and individuals step into their blessing to subdue the earth. And the promise is that, even though it seems so hit and miss nowadays, because of Jesus, one day this will all flow naturally in eternity!

Jesus' whole life is testimony to the power of the image of God before the world. And so it is no wonder that he said we will do even more than he did,[42] when we are all called into the same image of God identity.

So where does this leave us? We are more significant than we think we are - we are made to carry the same power and heart as God does; the whole of creation is there to serve us and to bless us. And yet we are also more insignificant than we think we are - we are who we are because of who God is. And therefore, God is even bigger than we give him credit for!

As I said earlier, to our 21st century sensibilities some of this can feel oppressive - dominion over

---

[42] John 14 v12

animals, and so forth - and not a blessing. But we need to recognise what God is inviting us into. These are the three primary behaviours of the image of God because these are the three primary behaviours of God, as established on page one.

God communes with Himself, He subdues the earth in preparation for life and then creates such an abundance of life.

Being the image of God is not about doing as we are told, being oppressed to follow instructions, which in turn oppress the world around us. We are not "commanded" to do the image of God stuff. It is about doing what God does. The image of God is marked by these three commissions and God calls them blessings, which we will carry out naturally if we live as He intended us to live, in relationship with him, reflecting and resonating him, so that his presence is found within us and his behaviour comes out from us.

These blessings mark our identity, our purpose and our potential, and they flow from an invitation: to walk with God, in the most intimate relationship between a father and His most beloved children.

We were created to live in that relationship - that is our natural state, the condition in which we will most naturally grow and find joy. Living as the image of God is about rediscovering our identity, not adopting a position of responsibility. It is about discovering that we are who we are because of who

God is, and not, as some would have it, the other way around.

And let's be in no doubt about how important this image identity is, both to God personally and to his plan for us and for creation as a whole, because the rest of God's Word is focused on tracing the story of the image of God, and reveals how far God had to go in order to safeguard it. This is one of the primary focuses of my next book, *The Eden Complex*, so I don't want to put too much of a spoiler in here, but suffice to say it began in Eden, where Adam initially lived out his calling as God's image, communing with God, subduing the earth and creating life. But then, disaster struck when he and Eve turned their eyes away from God and towards themselves.

It was a cataclysmic moment with three consequences for Adam and Eve, each reflecting their diminished ability to live as the image of God: the ground became harder to work, as the earth was harder to subdue, childbirth became more difficult and painful as it became harder to create life, and they were cast out of the garden, and it became harder to commune with God.

God's relationship with his people was terribly damaged, but it continued in diminished form and in his grace, God continued to live among his people, establishing first a covenant, opening up communion with him, then the Law, governing the preservation and pursuit of life, while at the same time working signs and wonders through angels and Godly men, subduing the earth.

185

This was the era of temporary grace for God's people, when the image of God was tarnished but still able to have some tangible meaning. Practically speaking, this fragile relationship was expressed first through prophetic encounters, then through the worship and sacrifice established in the tabernacle and finally the Temple. However, the people's uncleanness meant he could only live in limited sanctified space, be it a pillar of smoke and fire, a cloud over a mountain, or in a small room and even then only be visited under strict conditions. Even so, God considered the conditions worth it for the sake of continuing to live among his people.

However, his people's unholy ways continued to worsen so that even his room was tarnished and God was faced with a choice: to leave or to clean his house. The prospect of leaving was too terrible to contemplate, not only for himself, but it would have spelled eternal disaster for his beloved people, so after many prophetic warnings, he swept his house clean, as his people were sent away from his presence, into exile in Babylon. It was an act of grace and love, not harsh judgement, as he ensured his relationship with his people could be preserved and his promise to Abraham would be kept[43], and the way was now clear for God's ultimate act of loving sacrifice.

And then came Jesus, born into a time of prolonged distance between God and his people, and he

[43] Exodus 15

brought with him the Holy Spirit, as God returned to live among his people again. Jesus lived the perfect life as the image of God, communing with God intimately, subduing the earth powerfully and creating life liberally; claiming victory everywhere Adam and Eve had fallen to defeat. And after his extraordinary life, at the moment of his death on the cross, three momentous events occurred, all recorded by Matthew, in chapter 27, verses 51-53.

The first was that the temple curtain was torn from top to bottom, as communion with God was finally re-established. The second was that there was a tremendous earthquake, as the earth was subdued once more. The third was that the graves broke open, as life overtook death.

What happened in that moment was that Jesus, who had lived as the perfect image of God, as God had always intended for all of his people, extended his arms on the cross and offered the same opportunity to everyone. The consequences of Eden were finally swept aside and humanity was restored to its proper place in the eyes of creation.

Of course, this relied entirely on the purity and generosity of Jesus' sacrifice, and so our identity as the image of God today, as demonstrated throughout the rest of the New Testament, is freely available so long as we walk with God under the blood-stained banner of our Redeemer.

This is the meta-narrative of The Bible that I introduced in chapter one; this is the extent that God was willing to go to restore his vision for his people, to be made in his image, to live and work alongside him, to share in everything he has, to reflect and resonate him before all of creation. What an amazing, loving, graceful, merciful, awesome God we have! And what an amazing calling he has given us, and has given up everything so that we can receive!

So, perhaps this is an opportune moment to pause and consider how much of your life reflects that calling and invitation to be the image of God. Does your character, or your values, your priorities, your decisions or your hopes reveal a life set on communion with God, committed to creating life and willing to subdue the earth, lovingly as God does? Are you willing to do as he does, not because you can do it but because he can, not because of whom you are but because of whom he is?

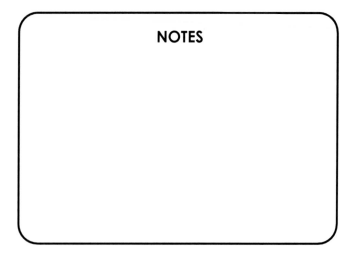

NOTES

NOTES

THE GOD OF PAGE ONE

12

THE
SEVENTH
DAY

And on the seventh day God finished his work that he had done, and he rested ...

Genesis 2 v 2

STUDY QUESTIONS (9)

Read Genesis 2 v 1-3.

What do we learn about God's character and priorities from the seventh day?

What is the natural rhythm God has initiated for life?

Key question: What makes the seventh day holy? How do we apply this to our own lives?

NOTES

OF COURSE, the creation account does not end at the completion of day six, no matter how much our modern-day chapter breaks appear to suggest otherwise. I am not entirely clear on why the seventh day is pushed back to the start of Genesis 2, but it is very much a part of the same account, which continues to reveal more of who God is:

Thus the heavens and the earth were finished, and all the host of them.
And on the seventh day God finished his work that he had done, and he rested on the seventh day from all his work that he had done. So God blessed the seventh day and made it holy, because on it God rested from all his work that he had done in creation.

Genesis 2 v 1-3

It is a wonderful thing to know that God knows when something is complete. It is clear that He saw what His creation was to become before the first day had begun, expressed in His naming the waters heaven and earth before they in any way reflected what God intended, and now they are complete - they are just as He had foreseen. And when God sees that something is complete, that it is very good, He is a God who declares that it is finished.

Here we have the culmination of an extraordinary journey, which has been explosive and yet intimate; which has involved sacrifice and separation, but also miracles and the initiation of a plan that will forever be God's most treasured priority: to be in relationship with us, and through us to be in relationship with all that He has made.

This is what He had always desired, and now it is finished and the heavens and the earth have stepped into the identity that God conferred upon them before they were formed. They have become what God always saw they would become, and what He had already declared they were.

It is such an encouragement to me that God thinks so highly of me that He calls me His child before I in any way resemble it, because He sees what I will become and that is sufficient for His grace to get me there.

It means so much to me that God is so attentive that He knows where I am on the journey of reflecting the identity He has already conferred upon me, and that when I finally stand in His presence He will know me so intimately that He can look me in the eye and say to me assuredly that I am complete.

That's how much he knows me, how much He loves me and how much He thinks of me.

Having affirmed that His work was finished, God rests. This is as much a part of the creative process as the preceding six days, and as much an integral part of God's nature as has been revealed in the excitement and action of His work.

We are not given the chance to think that God's nature is only revealed in what He does. What He does is shaped by who He is, not the other way round, and who He is extends beyond His work into his rest. In His rest there is no purpose to His existence except to live, and life is the most powerful, explosive, unstoppable, diverse and beautiful outcome of all of His work.

In other words, God's work always seeks to establish that which is most purely expressed in rest, and so rest is more than the recovery from work: it is the crowning glory of it, the goal that drives it, the measure of its completion.

Rest is the most inherently holy aspect of a life, because it is the state in which that life is celebrated for being beautiful, significant and important to God and His kingdom just as it is, without the conditions of getting it right or doing enough.

Rest is essential, revitalising, empowering, because it is in the place of rest that God is revealed purely for whom He is, and we are revealed for who we are.

Moreover, it is significant that it is God's seventh day and man's first. The crowning glory of God's work is to draw us into rest with Him, and the perfect place for us to work from is a place of rest with God.

In this way, the seventh day is as much about God establishing a pattern of life and the parameters for our relationship with Him as it is about putting time aside to have enough strength to work. In fact, this places work in its proper context - God's work is to draw us into resting in His presence, our work is to receive God's blessing in that place and carry it with us to the world.

Our work flows out of our rest. Or, as was so often a motto during my years at St Thomas' Philadelphia in Sheffield, we are to work from rest, not rest from work. On the whole, this is not something most of us are very good at. At least, I'm certainly not!

If we were to imagine our life as a graph with energy on the side 'y' axis and time along the bottom 'x' axis then most of us would probably relate to a pattern where we start at zero, or barely above it, so that as we work we drop to minus ten on our energy scale until we can bare it no longer; then we rest to get back as close to zero as we can in the time we have set aside.

This is not rest, but recovery, and recovery is not the promise of the seventh day. The graph only works if we start with rest, charging our energy from zero to plus ten so that when we work we can put our all into it as we work our way back down to zero, ready for our next time of rest.

In this rhythm of life charging our energy is about spending time in God's presence, coming to Him just as we are. He is the source of all life, and the giver of our identity, and so He is naturally the best source of restoration we have, in every area of our life. Practically speaking this is likely to involve time reflecting on His word, time in prayer, time in community with others in the church, and time doing the things we love, consciously inviting God to join us. After all, it's not called recreation (re-creation) for nothing!

So, what is it that gives you life? Time alone, time with friends, engaging with music or art, cooking, watching film or television, walking, sport, the possibilities are close to endless. Can it really be a holy thing to do these things? Of course! It was God who made you to come alive in that way, so of course He wants you to enjoy it and to share it with you!

This is the pattern of a life in balance. It is the rhythm of a life that is sent from and returns to God's presence, first receiving and then taking out God's Holy Spirit, His love and His transforming power; but even more importantly, this is the rhythm of a life that spends time in the company of the Heavenly Father, and discovers and celebrates who He has made them to be.

It is time drawing back into the vine, as Jesus put it in John 15. The more we live this life, the more we can detach our sense of our identity from the things we do and simply enjoy growing into being the people God foresaw when He first called us His child; and, according to Jesus' vine analogy, the more we live this life, the more fruitful we become.

This pattern of life is so important that every seventh day was singled out for special consideration - it was to be considered holy, not because it symbolised something great God did in the past, but because it was an invitation to engage in a godly rhythm of life now. Time away with God, in Sabbath rest, is a place of blessing.

Our God is a God who has set aside time to be with us. He prepared everything to be perfect for humanity before we got there, and when we arrived, He stopped working and we stepped into a day set aside for rest with Him; a time when relationship could be forged. Out of this God established a day's rest into our weekly rhythm, so that our time set aside with Him is regular and reliable, just as He is.

It is all about priorities. We see here a God who makes us His priority - builds a cosmos around us, steps back from such glorious work to spend time with us, and sends us out to rule over it, with the promise that so long as we prioritise Him, He will equip us with all we need.

Finally, at the end of this amazing, astonishing, action-packed, life-defining week, we discover a God who is holy.

We are told that God made the seventh day holy because on it He rested. Holiness means to be set apart, and it is measured by God's behaviour.

Whenever we rest we are taking part in Godly behaviour, as we set aside time to focus on being with Him and on being ourselves, not on our work, and God invites us to share that with Him in His holy Sabbath rest, where we are holy because we are joining in holy behaviour with the One who is holy.

THE GOD OF PAGE ONE

13

TAKING A STEP BACK

Thus the heavens and the earth were finished.

Genesis 2 v 1

SO, WHO is God? We have only read the first chapter of The Bible, but by the end of Genesis 1 we know so much about our maker. We also know a good deal about who He has made us to be and how we are to relate to Him, all crystallised in the wonderful revelation that He has created us in the image of God.

However, as we come to the end of our Genesis 1 exploration, let us finish as we began: reflecting on the first and most fundamental question that The Bible always endeavours to answer: who is God? What have we discovered from page one?

Well, we know that ...

Our God is a creator.

He is eternal and He is powerful.

He is loving.

He is relational.

He invites those in relationship with Him into His work.

He is a story-teller.

He has a plan, and His plan is perfect and resplendent in precision.

He wants us to see and share and delight in His creation.

He draws light from the dark places but is still present in the darkness.

He reveals and is a revelation.

He is a guide.

He gives identity and purpose.

His voice releases His power and it invites us towards Him.

He is the King of Kings.

He is sacrificial.

He hates to be separated from His creation and from us.

He sees further than we do and He works all things for good.

He elevates us.

He yearns for intimacy.

He understands our needs and He meets them.

He is our provider.

He is wise.

He loves variety.

He is beautiful.

He is complex.

Everything and everyone matters to Him.

He will go to any lengths to equip and bless the world and the people He loves so much.

He works in seasons.

His blessing is abundant.

He is humble.

He is the source of all life.

He is generous.

He knows us intimately and knows everything we face.

He invites us to share everything He has and holds nothing back.

He is our protector.

He is reliable.

He completes what He starts.

He is attentive.

He rests.

He makes time to be with us.

He is holy.

He is very good ...

... and He is our dad.

This is the God of page one, this is who He is, this is what He is like, this is what He does, and we are who we are because of who He is. His story already impacts our story and will do so even more in the pages to come.

THE GOD OF PAGE ONE

You have met God, says page one. Do you want to hear His story?

Then read on ...

About the author

Freddy Hedley is Training Director at Fountain of Life Church, Ashill, where he also serves as the Director for New Wine Training in East Anglia. He is also a part of the Anglican Church Planting Initiatives (ACPI) team and is a Fresh Expressions Associate Missioner. His passion is to see people excited and inspired by God's Word in new ways and to apply that enthusiasm to their life and witness. His published works include *Listening for Mission*, *Lessons from Antioch*, *Coaching for Missional Leadership* and *Walking in Freedom*. He lives in Norfolk with his wife Ali and two young (and very loud!) daughters.

Other books published by Emblem Books

Lessons from Antioch The church in Antioch is one of the most fruitful and effective examples of a community of faith recorded in the New Testament. With so much inspiration coming out of this church, whose mission context relates so much to ours, surely there are lessons we can learn that will impact how we seek to engage with God's missionary call to the church today.

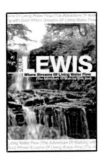

Where Streams of Living Water Flow is part journal, part autobiography and part survival guide. It is the true story of a man who embarked on an adventure with a thirst to hear from God. Jargon-free and written from the heart, this is one man's quest to discover the joy of intimacy with God as Jesus invited us to drink the living water only he offers.

Love Each Other God has called us into something quite distinct from anything else in the world, something that the New Testament calls the common life or fellowship. This was perhaps the most attractive feature of the life of the Early Church and is something we need to recapture today. This book explores how we can learn afresh to Love Each Other in the 21st century.

Lightning Source UK Ltd.
Milton Keynes UK
UKOW01f1341150616

276270UK00002B/16/P